20°

IONIAN SEA

GREECE

Sporades
Islands

AEGEAN
SEA

TURKEY

40°

Ionian
Islands

Euboea

Athens

of Messina

Cyclades
Islands

Dodecanese
Islands

Rhodes

CRETE

ERRANEAN SEA

ALTERING COURSE

ALTERING COURSE

RICHARD J. VOGT

Preface by Roderick Stephens Jr.

Foreword by Arthur Beiser

Charts by Miriam Schiff Hersey

COLOR PHOTOGRAPHS BY DAN NERNEY

Sail Books, Inc.

BOSTON

Library of Congress Cataloging in Publication Data:

Vogt, Richard J.
    Altering Course.

    1. Mischief (Sailboat) 2. Vogt, Richard J.
    3. Voyages and travels—1951-   I. Title.
    G470.V73   910'.41'0924 B   78-8196
    ISBN 0-914814-12-5

*To Gayle, rarest of all jewels,
a congenial seagoing wife.*

Contents

Preface

by Roderick Stephens Jr.

This saga of *Mischief* cannot be fully enjoyed or appreciated without a reader's becoming at least a little acquainted with those who were primarily responsible. As I think back on *Mischief*'s beginnings after a span of some nine years, the essentials still stand out sharply and clearly in my mind.

On a day in May, 1969, I had an office appointment to meet with a Mr. and Mrs. Richard J. Vogt from Miami, who were interested in the possibility of a new design. As is usual at such preliminaries, I was hoping that the people I was about to meet would be pleasant, and above all that they would have a reasonably definite idea of what they might wish Sparkman and Stephens to produce. This last characteristic, I further hoped, would be combined with a willingness to listen favorably to our own suggestions, which can on some occasions be rather difficult to get across.

From this viewpoint, the initial meeting was filled with great promise. Dick Vogt and his lovely wife, Gayle, were delightful people, and on top of that, they had their "ducks all in a row." Their groundwork for our meeting could not have been more completely and correctly prepared.

Dick had no difficulty in outlining what their targets were, which he backed up with the specific design parameters described within this book. In addition to these clearly stated requisites, he had a voluminous—and happily legible—notebook which pre-answered a great majority of the questions that come up in the preparation of a new design.

As the project developed, I was pleased to learn that Gayle's contribution was not by any means limited to decoration (which was superbly handled) but that in addition she had clear and concise opinions when they were solicited. Even more fortunately, these didn't ever conflict with the wishes of her husband or the recommendations of designers.

Another welcome circumstance was that the tentative schedule gave us ample time to work the project over carefully. We would be able to review thoroughly the many variables that any important project presents, thus permitting intelligent decisions on the innumerable compromises and trade-offs that must always be made.

It certainly is not unusual for a good sailor to have a pretty firm idea, down to minute details, of what he or she wants and what is required. Judging from the amount and excellence of detailed requirements he had compiled, we could tell that Dick Vogt had done his homework painstakingly. The reader perhaps will be interested here to sample some outstanding design requirements, and to learn how they were solved.

One was the problem of the stowage on deck of an eight-foot fiberglass dinghy shaped like a Boston Whaler (it was, in fact, a "Perfection 8"). This was of such concern to Dick that he did not commit himself to a new design from Sparkman and Stephens until this single important problem was solved. He and I and my associate, Frank Kinney, all agreed that the best place for the dinghy was the afterdeck behind the mizzen mast. But on a yawl of the proposed size of *Mischief*, the afterdeck is not long enough, so we suggested a boomkin of aluminum pipe, continuing the deck line in plain view aft to an elliptical end.

The boomkin was intended only to gain space. There remained the problems of how to hoist the dinghy, how to stow it, and how to launch it. At first we proposed the solution of using the mizzen halyard, but in this case it had to be rejected because the top of the mizzen was only about 26 feet above the deck. Frank Kinney came up with the idea of utilizing a mainsheet track slide and block, securing it upside-down in the underside of the mizzen boom. A tag line forward and another one aft would allow it to function as a crane. The concept pleased Dick Vogt immensely, and he then told us to go ahead with the whole design.

Another requirement that concerned us was carrying and stowing six anchors. Not one of our other 2,300 designs had called for so many. Dick insisted on it, however, because of anchoring problems in the Bahamas, where a boat must be anchored fore and aft so as not to swing out of a deep hole when the current reverses. We put our minds to it and came up with the following pattern: (1) a 45-lb. plow in a roller chock on the port side of the bowsprit, (2) a 20-lb. Danforth on the hood of the fo'c's'le sliding hatch, (3) a 60-lb. Danforth lashed standing up on deck to the port main shroud, (4) a 40-lb. kedge anchor in three pieces stowed alongside the fo'c's'le hatch. Below decks are stowed (5) a 13-lb. Northill and (6) a 75-lb. three-piece anchor, both in the starboard lazarette.

A third unusual requirement was a rudder detail. Dick Vogt wanted the automatic pilot to be able to steer a tab at the trailing edge of the rudder, so that less power would be consumed. Our experiment with this, quite frankly, did not wholly succeed in steering the boat automatically in all conditions of wind and sea. We developed a 3″

(O.D.) rudder stock out of 3/8"-thick aluminum; inside this was a 1" stainless steel shaft with linkage to turn the tab without turning the rudder. Perhaps it failed to perform well under all conditions because the tab was located in turbulent water disturbed by the propeller's aperture. In any event, it wasn't because the tab was too small, since we later increased its length to no significant effect.

A fourth design criterion—lots of space inside—was made possible largely by *Mischief*'s aluminum construction, which allowed for integral tanks. It was a delightful fringe benefit that the execution of this welded aluminum alloy hull was so beautifully performed by Wolter Huisman's Overijsselse Jachtwerf at Vollenhove in Holland.

Adding further to the success of the project was Frans Maas of Breskens, who did a magnificent job in the finishing, expeditiously and skillfully getting it all together, including the unusual and voluminous storage requirements that were to be needed for long-distance sailing and for living on board.

The collective significance of all this is quite apparent as one follows *Mischief*'s wanderings herein. It certainly adds tremendously to both the safety and the pleasure of long-distance cruising when one has on board just about everything that is, or might be, required, even under the most unexpected of circumstances. *Mischief*'s sailing trials were completed on July 3, 1972—some three years and three months after the date of our first meeting in New York—and her story surely underscores the happy fruits of our collaboration.

NEW YORK CITY
MARCH 1978

12

Foreword

by Arthur Beiser

In the course of preparing a new edition of my book *The Proper Yacht*, I spent a morning not long ago with Olin Stephens to discuss cruising sailboats in general and recent ones from his office in particular. One of his favorites among the latter was Dick Vogt's *Mischief III*, which interested me not only because she is a fine vessel but also because she is a member of a fast-vanishing species, the one-off cruising boat of moderate size.

The custom construction of almost anything is wildly uneconomic these days, which makes Mr. Vogt all the more to be envied, since *Mischief* was built just before the latest surge in building costs. To emulate Mr. Vogt's once-normal approach—first defining his goals carefully, then working with a designer to get everything he wanted in a harmonious package, and finally having the resulting lines on paper transmuted into a splendid boat—is possible for very few people any longer. On the other hand, stock fiberglass boats in all sizes are available at prices well under those for comparable custom boats. But not many experienced cruising sailors will find their dream boats among them, and it is not always easy to decide what to insist upon and where to accept a compromise. Since production and marketing considerations did not enter into the design of *Mischief*, the solutions she embodies to the problems of wind and sea, close-quarters living, and so on are worth a close look by anyone contemplating a new boat.

A number of factors influence the lower limit to the size of a proper cruising boat. One of them is the need for enough room for the usual crew to live aboard without strain. Another is the ability to carry water, fuel, and supplies for an ocean crossing. Even if such a crossing is not part of one's plans for a boat, the required self-sufficiency is good to have. Small boats are less stable than large ones, which means more sail changing and more effort needed to carry out a given task. Finally, size means speed, and sailing fast is fun. Because people vary in their tolerance of discomfort and of other boats sailing past them, the lower limit is not sharp, but for me it is around a displacement of 15,000 pounds, say 26 feet on the waterline.

The upper end of the size range for a proper yacht is set by the requirement that a man and a woman be able to handle it themselves on a coastwise cruise. If they cannot, then they are the slaves of their guests or paid hands, apart from being denied the pleasure of sailing by themselves. Even though such modern blessings as multispeed winches, roller-furling jibs, power windlasses, and self-stowing anchors make a squad of gorillas unnecessary on a large sailboat if all goes well, all sometimes does not go well. Past a displacement of 45,000 pounds or so, perhaps 40 feet on the waterline, sails and anchors begin to be big fellows, and if a strong wind is present, bringing a large boat into a harbor berth with just a man and a woman on board may be the most taxing job of all.

With a waterline length of 32 feet, *Mischief* is well away from both extremes of size. Large enough to be fast and steady under way, she is also small enough not to press her crew unduly. *Mischief*'s displacement of 26,600 pounds is close to optimum for a cruising boat of her waterline length, since it enables robust construction and ample carrying capacity without handicapping her sailing ability more than a trifle. Boats light for their length can be exhilarating to sail under the right conditions, but place too many demands on their crews and are too intolerant of heavy loads to be good as cruisers. Ultraheavy boats are great for living on board, not so great when it comes to going places.

It is my impression after many years of sailing on both sides of the Atlantic that the number of accessible harbors doubles with every reduction in draft of two feet. Hence *Mischief,* which draws 4 feet 3 inches with her centerboard up, can get into about three times as many places as can a fin-keeled IOR racer of her size. (This is no exaggeration; it may even be an underestimate.) Because shoal-draft keel boats do not sparkle to windward, the only way to combine all-around ability under sail with the capacity to cruise anywhere is to have a centerboard. The objection is sometimes raised that a centerboard is a potential source of trouble and so does not belong in a serious vessel. However, the two most experienced cruising sailors I know, Irving Johnson and Jim Crawford, had their most recent boats equipped with centerboards, and both *Yankee* and *Angantyr* have survived tens of thousands of miles without embarrassment. So Dick Vogt is in good company. Still, having a centerboard is not without penalty even at best. Probably the main disadvantage, apart from the extra cost, is the lack of a deep bilge well. If even a modest volume of water enters the hull for any reason, it can be a real nuisance when the boat heels by getting into berths and stowage areas.

Mischief has a modern, efficient hull form. Why does she not ape the Colin Archers, Friendship sloops, or Itchen ferries of the past that are so dear to the hearts of a certain segment of the yachting fraternity? The answer is that *Mischief* was designed for cruising under sail, not as a tugboat for distressed Lofoten fishermen, a lobster-pot tender, or a jitney ferryboat. She is just as nicely matched to her task today as they were to theirs in their day, and unless Mr. Vogt falls on hard times and needs to make a living by rescuing fishermen, catching lobsters, or delivering fancy ladies to anchored ships, he has no reason to regret his choice.

Aluminum is used for *Mischief*'s entire body shell, in my opinion the best available material for the purpose. Aluminum combines strength, durability, and lightness, permits integral tanks, and facilitates a centerboard installation. Alas, aluminum is not as suitable as fiberglass for series production, which puts it out of reach for most sailors today.

Like her hull, *Mischief*'s rig is not in accord with the IOR-influenced fashions of the moment. Her sail plan is broken up into four separate units—jib, forestaysail, mainsail, and mizzen—which means that the area and balance of the sails can be adjusted with minimum labor to suit changing conditions. My 58-foot ketch *Minots Light* has a similar rig, and I cannot imagine a handier arrangement for a big boat. However, *Mischief* is not all that big, and I wonder whether a cutter rig might not suit her better. Her performance to windward and downwind in light weather would benefit, and light airs are vastly more common than squalls on most cruises. In any case, a good jiffy-reefing system would make shortening down no more trouble than dropping the main or mizzen. Eliminating the mizzen would get rid of a lot of windage and allow a vane self-steerer to be installed, a most desirable feature on a bluewater cruiser. As a cutter, *Mischief* would need neither bowsprit nor boomkin. But my objection is a mild one; it is as important that a rig suit the owner as that it suit the boat, and if Mr. Vogt prefers *Mischief* as a yawl, then that is the rig she should have.

The sizes of wire and hardware used on *Mischief*'s

standing rigging are generous for her size, which reduces the likelihood of fatigue failure on a long voyage by minimizing the stresses they experience. To an engineer, stress is force per unit cross-sectional area, so for a given force, the thicker the object acted upon, the smaller the stress. The smaller the stress, in turn, the greater the number of stress cycles that can occur before fatigue failure becomes likely. The effect is not linear: an "oversize" fitting that seldom experiences a stress of more than, say, 10 percent of its breaking strength when new is apt to survive hundreds of times more cycles than one that is regularly stressed to 30 or 40 percent of its original strength, which might otherwise seem to leave an ample safety margin. The additional weight and windage aloft of *Mischief*'s rigging are entirely acceptable in view of the greater long-term security they afford, which is equally true for the double spreaders on her mainmast and the triatic stay between her mastheads.

Mischief's after cabin provides sleeping quarters in the most stable part of the boat out of the way of all the various activities that occur in the accommodation on a passage. Nobody cooks, eats, navigates, plays pinochle, sheds wet oilies, rummages for tools or shackles, or stores sails there. To keep this oasis of calm and order free of traffic, the main companionway was located on top of the cabin house, which also cuts the risk of flooding in case of a knockdown. Unfortunately such an arrangement isolates the cockpit from the accommodation and makes communicating with the chart table difficult. A midships cockpit would permit the same degree of separation of the after cabin but would better integrate life in the cockpit with life down below. However, in a boat this size more would be lost than gained by adopting a midships cockpit, since it would take up space in the widest part of the hull that can ill be spared. With four to six feet more of waterline length, the balance might well go the other way, but for

Mischief the tradeoff that was chosen seems to have been the most sensible.

Chart table, oilie locker, and galley flank the companionway, as they should, with the sink as close as possible to the centerline so it can drain on both tacks. I like having the head compartment in this region too, so that someone on deck can get to it without having to trail seawater through the main cabin or alternatively waste effort in removing and putting back on wet oilies and seaboots. Incorporating a toilet and washbasin in the forward cabin is another excellent idea. Any cruising boat of this size ought to have two heads, but if the normal complement will not exceed six, having one of them as part of a cabin is a good way to save space. The only improvement I can think of would be to have a door to the main head directly from the after cabin, but the available room seems insufficient. Six inches here, a foot there would make many things easier—but then the boat would be longer, wider, deeper, and heavier, would need a larger rig and engine, and would end up a different boat entirely.

An ideal main cabin for passagemaking would feature pilot berths outboard of both settees, so that two people can sack out there without interfering with others eating or lounging. With a total of six on board, all four guests could sleep in the main cabin when the owners are on deck if the forward cabin proved uninhabitable at the time. On the other hand, to have fixed pilot berths on both sides without unduly cramping the rest of the cabin means a lot of beam, and it also means giving up useful shelf and locker space. *Mischief*'s main cabin compromises by including just one pilot berth with a backrest that converts to an upper on the other side. A quite reasonable solution. Another would be to have narrow pilot berths that can be extended to sleeping width by folding down their fronts and inserting supplementary mattress sections. Which arrangement is better naturally depends on how often the boat is sailed offshore and with how large a crew.

Foreword

Mischief's tanks hold 180 gallons of water and 140 of diesel oil, not bad for a shoal hull 32 feet on the waterline. On the basis of a gallon of water per person per day, which means being careful but not obsessive about water consumption, 180 gallons will last a crew of six for nearly 30 days, a crew of four for nearly 45. A comfortable amount for ocean cruising, more than enough for coastwise cruising. The fuel capacity seems adequate for a range under power of at least 1300 miles at a speed in the neighborhood of 6 knots. With room for stores and spares plus a real workbench, *Mischief* has enough autonomy for any venture her owner might wish to undertake.

In discussing *Mischief,* the word compromise is inevitable in most departments. Yet *Mischief* as a whole is not a compromise, such is the good sense that has governed each decision. She is a proper yacht, and given her solid construction, is likely to remain one for decades to come. The same can be said about a few of the stock fiberglass boats on the market today, and no doubt their proportion will increase as prospective owners learn to concentrate on basics and not on number of berths or upholstery patterns in assessing their merits.

ÎLE DES EMBIEZ
MAY 1977

"Believe me, my young friends, [said the Water Rat,] there is *nothing*—absolutely nothing—half so much worth doing as simply messing about in boats. Simply messing. . . . Nothing seems really to matter, that's the charm of it. Whether you get away, or whether you don't; whether you arrive at your destination or whether you reach somewhere else, or whether you never get anywhere at all, you're always busy, and you never do anything in particular. . . ."

from Kenneth Grahame, *The Wind in the Willows*

1

Prologue

It is difficult to define exactly when *Mischief*'s saga begins. Was it that August day when she first poked her bows into the waves from the little fishing port of Breskens, Holland? Or was it really much earlier, at some indefinite point in my musings over a span of decades when I would be sailing her in fantasy?

The dream I had long held was to voyage afar in a sailing boat; to see people and places in a manner possible only by this means; to move in humble harmony with the sea and the wind and to count these formidable elements as my friends. In this way of life I expected to encounter new experiences and people, to discover new values, and to enrich my life.

With *Mischief,* Gayle and I together have found these things, and we have discovered a wholesome new quality of personal well-being difficult to describe but very real and satisfying. We have eliminated much of the superficial clutter from our lives. This includes thinking habits as well as living habits. Living on the boat has made both of us healthier, mentally and physically. In a push-button era one can easily lose the ability to take care of oneself, even in the simplest ways. Self-sufficiency, independence, mobility, and simplicity of living on a boat are satisfactions we consciously savor every day. Moreover, we have been forced to learn new skills, and as a result we have become involved in many new fields of knowledge—navigation, weather, mechanics, radio, oceanography, to name a few in a long list of shipboard concerns. But no matter how unfamiliar our circumstances or surroundings may be, we are always home. In a strange country we always can sleep in our own beds.

In my adult life I think I have always had in me quite a bit of the Puritan ethic—hard work, devotion to duty, steadfast principles, conventional habits and tastes, and such. But also I have been at heart an adventurer and beachcomber with a kinship for the sea. This latter side of my personality was for a long time reconciled to the former; perhaps "subjugated" is a more appropriate term.

At the age of 59, however, I came to a decision that it was time I implemented my dream. I then held, as I had for some years, an interesting position as Senior Vice-President of a large bank holding company, a multi-billion-dollar Florida giant of international reputation, with its stock listed on the New York Stock Exchange. To realize my dream of sailing was a personal decision of vital importance, for it meant pulling up deep roots. It was a crucial decision as well for my wife, who was an associate professor of history at the University of Miami.

Together and in full agreement we committed ourselves, thoughtfully and quietly. Our children accepted the news without really being surprised, knowing folk that they are. I was significantly encouraged by my personal physician, a friend who warranted this change in my way of life would be conducive to good health and longevity. My close business associates and friends and Gayle's colleagues at the university were sometimes incredulous, but many gradually came to regard our unfolding plan with undisguised envy.

Gayle and I had been married in what might be called late middle-life and had brought two grown families together. Our collective four children were responsible young adults, three of them married. They had settled in distant communities and were building their own worlds in the normal evolution of things. They had produced numerous grandchildren in whom we all delighted. We owned a pleasant bay-front home in Coconut Grove where we lived, had a comfortably modest accumulation of stocks and bonds, a couple of automobiles and a handsome 36-foot steel yawl. We belonged to a number of local clubs, including a yacht club where I had been Commodore for a time. We vacationed in the nearby Bahamas on our boat, and weekended as often as possible in the Florida Keys. Gayle owned a Blue Jay, which she and one of our daughters sometimes raced. Ocean racing had more appeal to me than "around-the-buoys" courses and for many years I raced as crewman or navigator in annual Southern Ocean Racing Conference events.

For many people in these circumstances, it would be easy to dream and let it go at that, or to dream and say "five more years" or "three more years" or even "one more year." But Gayle and I modestly claim to be young for our years, and we are blessed with good health. So we made the decision to act now to implement the dream—to satisfy a deep longing for the sea. We have never regretted this decision.

2

Implementing the dream

The success of any project tends to match the effectiveness of its planning. Our plans were laid with care and forethought. With this—and a little luck—things fell into place for us as we converted to what, in due course, would be a new life-style at sea.

In the spring of 1969 our implementation of the dream to go to sea involved five areas of decision, all intricately related and requiring careful coordination. (For example, it would have been irresponsible to get in over our heads financially; inconvenient to be retired on reduced income before the boat was finished, or vice versa; catastrophic to find ourselves disenchanted after having committed so much effort, thought, and money to fulfilling the dream; unwise not to have retained some reversible options.) The five areas were:

- Financial feasibility and flexibility of the whole idea.
- Disengagement from business, professional, and community interests.
- Financial planning details and controls for our guidance during and after the transition.

- Determining basic requirements in a new boat and its probable or permissive cost.
- Acquiring the boat.

Clearly the first requirement would be to satisfy ourselves that the project was financially feasible, and its irreversible aspects acceptable. We resolved the latter by discussion. The former required forecasting what our practical options would be, the probable amount and sources of capital and income available, what factors would cause significant variations in these amounts, the importance of timing, and the degree of control I could reasonably exert over such factors.

I worked out a series of alternate plans, each programming the use of capital resouces to accomplish the objective, and of course each related to future income and expense requirements. Purely on general principle rather than any actual reservations, we agreed that reasonable conditions of reversibility would be essential; this would be important in case of a serious injury, illness, or death. Thus we decided to make the investment in the boat a generally recoverable one. I set a range within which to control this investment, and workable budgets of income and expense for future guidance.

Our disengagement from business, professional, and community interests required obvious forethought. We had to balance our self-interest with responsibilities we had accepted and the need for an orderly change. I notified the board of directors and my business associates of the decision to elect early retirement at the optional age of 62, then three years away. This provided adequate lead-time for management succession. Two years later Gayle resigned as associate professor of history at the University of Miami, a position she had held for nine years, irrevocably yielding her tenure. I finally retired at the end of 1972 nearing my sixty-third birthday.

Thus, pinning down the business and financial aspects

of our dream took three and a half years. In retrospect I think it was wholesome not to rush things along too fast, allowing time for second thoughts, if any. The planning, design and construction of the new *Mischief* also took a little over three years, which suited us admirably.

In May, 1969, Gayle and I had our first meeting with Roderick Stephens Jr. of Sparkman & Stephens, Inc., in New York for a preliminary talk about a possible new boat. We had not yet chosen from several courses which lay open to us. The choices were somewhat obvious, but to be thorough we wanted to evaluate each of them over a period of time. Here, in brief, are the choices we considered:

1. Keep our present boat and modify her as required. This boat was a 36' Zeeland-class yawl we had owned for 14 years since she was new. Her steel hull was sound and the boat well maintained. She would need additional equipment for extended offshore service and interior alterations to be more liveable for a not-as-young-as-we-used-to-be couple. Remodeling usually is a costly procedure, and of course there are design limits on what one can do. With the help of yard estimates, we were not long in deciding that this cost would be prohibitive considering the value of the boat, it would not add significantly to a future resale value, and it would fall short of our ideal design.

2. Find a used boat of sound and attractive design. This was an appealing alternative, but for us it meant shopping in Europe. The best market for cruising-design sailboats then was England. Until recent years American builders have been preoccupied with production racing/cruising designs, neglecting the pure cruising market.

Aside from the inconvenience of shopping in Europe, there was the awkward problem of what to do with a boat we might find abroad, for we would still be tied down at home with our job-disengagement countdowns. We would also undoubtedly be faced with costly design modifications. Moreover, any older boat, such as our Zeeland yawl, was apt to require heavy maintenance.

3. Buy a good stock boat new, and modify her to suit our needs. This offered interesting possibilities at first, but as we got down to specifics we found it impractical. Some contrary views notwithstanding, it is my opinion that modifications in original stock designs are in most cases superficial; moreover, they do not significantly increase the market value of a boat, and might even detract from it. Thus the considerable cost would be unrecoverable, and it might be better in all respects to start from the beginning.

At that time we could not find any stock boats on the market which were really designed for offshore service, except some European motor-sailer designs. Happily for the cruising sailor, this situation has changed in subsequent years, and some interesting stock cruising boats are now available. But at that time, we had to rule out this choice as impractical, unsatisfactory, and a poor investment.

4. Build a new custom-design boat. This possibility was a temptation from the time we first discarded the idea of modifying our old boat. This would undoubtedly be our last boat, and in light of the alternatives available, we were tempted to make it the best we could afford. She could fit our needs and specifications exactly; she could be a thing of quality and beauty. If well done, a custom-designed yacht could be an outstanding vessel and thus a sound, if large, investment, especially in this age of world-wide inflation. There is always a market for a diamond!

In the end we elected to follow the custom-design alternative. However logical I have made this decision appear, I am frank to say it was partly an emotional one. We sold our old boat, though it took over a year and some price concessions to do so. We sold our home in Coconut Grove, Florida, waiting patiently two and a half years to get our asking price, put our furniture into storage, and rented an apartment in nearby Key Biscayne.

Sparkman & Stephens would be the designers. In due course—about eighteen months later—the design and specifications were complete. How much it would cost to build such a boat was, at this point, only an informed guess. Bids were now in order, and until the cost could be ascertained definitely, I stood ready to abort the entire project if it seemed prudent to do so.

Invitations to bid were sent on our behalf by Sparkman & Stephens to qualified builders in the United States and abroad. Typical replies were, "To build a yacht to the specifications of your design #2040 we bid [so much] for delivery in [so many] months at [wherever]." We did have some surprises in the bidding, which ranged shockingly wide, the low being 40 percent below the high. But the low was in our ball-park, and we excitedly moved into the final stage of acquiring our dream boat.

The Frans Maas yard in Holland was low bidder and our enthusiastic choice in other respects as well. Our previous boat also had been of Dutch build and design, and was a great satisfaction. The Dutch had not named a delivery time, indicating their de-emphasis of production scheduling. The final contract, payable in guilders, specified delivery in one year. This was perfectly adequate for us, although it was twice as long as other builders had offered. Rod Stephens, experienced in coping with this Dutch characteristic, even commented, "You wouldn't hold them to this date, would you?" Within reason, of course, I would not; but exactly one year after construction started, sea trials were held, and two months later we sailed away in a reasonably shaken-down and de-bugged new boat.

Financial aspects of such an overseas project posed no problem, but certain terms of the contract and the mechanics of payment may be of interest. It was October, 1970, when the Maas bid was accepted. However, I faced an awkward time interval, for I would not be able to take possession of the new boat in Europe by October, 1971, because of business commitments. My scheduled retirement was to be in mid-1972. The builder's bid could not be held open unreasonably because costs already were escalating under the pull of inflation.

This problem was resolved satisfactorily by negotiation. We signed a conditional contract at the bid price, with a delayed starting date for construction. We included a small payment to bind the contract, forfeitable if the balance of the initial one-third starting payment was not made by a specified starting date in mid-1971. Thus the yard would find it worthwhile to hold space for this order within its limited construction capacity, and I would not have to submit to the uncertainty of another round of bidding later.

As we neared the starting date, I purchased Dutch guilders from my Miami bank, instructing the bank to transmit these funds to a designated Amsterdam bank for credit to my account. Periodically I drew checks payable in guilders, and later used the account for convenience when *Mischief* cruised abroad. Some of this money was placed in an interest-bearing deposit in Amsterdam until it was needed. Also I arranged with the Amsterdam bank for a line of unsecured credit to be available on the customary European overdraft basis during the construction of the boat. This was in case the second progress payment should come due at an inopportune time.

During this period the dollar was declining in value against stronger European currencies, such as the guilder. The cost of buying guilders with dollars began to rise. Worse yet, I suspected official devaluation might come before long. To protect myself from escalating guilder costs on a fixed-price guilder contract with the builder, I covered the second one-third progress payment ahead of time (at some personal inconvenience, as we had not yet sold the house or the old boat) at a guilder price about 10 percent above the initial rate. These funds also were placed at interest in Amsterdam until needed.

Dollar devaluation subsequently occurred twice during construction, and exchange markets were sorely disrupted. Despite my preparations for this, the final payment for the same amount in guilders still cost about 20 percent more than the first. Since then the guilder has risen considerably more against the dollar, for a total increase of 50 percent in seven years from the original construction contract date in 1970! Of course, the cost of building a boat anywhere has shot up substantially with inflation.

In hindsight, the investment in the new *Mischief* was one of the best I ever made from a strict money-value standpoint, even without regard to the intangible returns on this investment. My decision to have the investment in the boat largely recoverable was fulfilled by a combination of luck, good management, and the completion of an outstanding design. Four years and nearly 20,000 miles after commissioning, *Mischief* was insured at 80 percent of her surveyed replacement cost, which, in turn, was 175 percent above original cost. She was in mint condition, and we keep her that way largely through our own efforts.

3

Mischief

Anyone thinking about building or buying a sailboat for offshore cruising may be interested to know how we went about it. Not that he will necessarily follow the same path, but here and there our experience surely will be helpful.

In early conferences with Sparkman & Stephens, Gayle and I laid down our personal plans in general terms. We wanted to sail afar, short-handed, and be safe and comfortable in the process. In rough fashion we established initial design guidelines, then added specifics. Of course I had rather clear ideas of what I wanted in a boat, but I did not wish to hamper the architect's innovativeness. To impose one's own ideas unduly could turn out to be shortsighted. To allow Sparkman & Stephens complete design control, on the other hand, would mean that our boat would be what *they* wanted it to be rather than what we wanted.

We were soon to discover that working with S & S would be both pleasant and effective. The success of the design would later speak for itself through the boat. But had no boat emerged in reality from the design drawings and specifications, the experience of creating a fine yacht.

if only on paper, would have been a uniquely stimulating one.

The concept of *Mischief* really began some 25 years before when I started keeping a notebook on what I considered to be my ultimate cruising boat. In it I accumulated scores of ideas, sketches, and notes. The designers borrowed it, to my surprise, and transcribed it in full. Later, when vaguely familiar details began to emerge from their drawing boards, I realized why these details elicited my instant approval: they were entries in my notebook, often expanded or improved.

More generally, I put down on paper some broad guidelines for all of us to keep in mind. I drew up five design criteria which I wanted the architect to follow. These were listed in order of priority, but I considered the last almost as important as the first.

1. The yacht should be strong enough to be able to stand to almost any sea.
2. She should be of such size and rig as to be easily handled by two people.
3. She should be big enough to provide comfortable living aboard for two people for extended periods, and occasionally four.
4. She should be a craft of special beauty.
5. She should be fast and smart under sail without regard to the design constraints of the racing rules.

Of course, I was simply describing the perfect cruising boat. Still, these were tangible objectives, and they became useful guides for decision-making throughout the design stage. Needless to say, S & S particularly liked "design parameter #5," as it gave them a rare freedom in this aspect of design technology. Happily, *Mischief* was to meet all my design criteria.

I had to agree with the designer on certain basics. Design fees, for example, would be on a time basis with no minimum, so the project could be aborted at any point.

All materials and specifications would be of the highest quality. Systems and equipment would be designed to be as simple and fail-safe as possible, so that maintenance would be low.

A divided rig was an early and unanimous choice for our offshore cruising yacht. It would permit more flexibility in design and use of the sail plan, with less dependence upon the mainsail. We favored a yawl with a generous mizzen over a ketch. The larger mizzen of the latter would need to be reefed to balance a working headsail when the main was reefed or not carried, or when the main was replaced by a storm trysail. And extra sail-handling is usually required when least welcome. *Mischief* would balance perfectly with mizzen and staysail, with or without storm trysail or reefed main. Moreover, a yawl rig would free the cockpit from having to accommodate the mizzen mast, providing either more usable cockpit space or a smaller cockpit area. Additionally, with a larger percentage of the designed sail area forward, other things being equal, a yawl has better windward ability than a ketch.

We also made an early choice of the structural material to be used: whether wood, fiberglass, or metal. I have a bias for metal, specifically steel because of its strength, but the extra weight of a steel boat tends to reduce performance under sail. We considered wood and ruled it out because of higher maintenance. Thus the choice came down to fiberglass or aluminum. Plans and specifications were drawn for aluminum construction, although in the final contract bidding one builder offered an alternate bid in one-off sandwich fiberglass construction at a saving of 10 percent in total cost.

Those who consider the initial cost of aluminum construction to be excessive may not be aware of its ultimate strength-for-weight advantage: S & S engineers calculated that to build in fiberglass, matching the stress and impact strength of aluminum alloy would increase the total weight significantly. This is why we selected aluminum over fiberglass—Alcoa 3083H32 and 5086H32 alloys, to be exact. These alloys may well be the best seagoing structural materials for yachts yet devised.

The objective of low maintenance and uncomplicated gear is a principle with which almost anyone would agree, yet in practice many boat owners do otherwise—they burden themselves with gadgets. While *Mischief* may seem to have everything, there are many things she does not have, for reasons of reliability and safety. A lot of gear on a yacht can be operated by hand as well as electrically. In general when the choice occurred, we elected the former. Electrical gear we did choose had hand-operated back-up systems—pressure water, for example.

I set a policy, as a matter of fact, that within practical limits every system that would be essential either to safety or comfort should have a back-up. The end result has been a high degree of operational reliability at sea. In the hostile environment of damp salt air, equipment failures are inevitable, as every boat-owner knows. *Mischief*'s failures have been fewer in number because of her uncomplicated systems, and of less consequence because back-ups were designed for stand-by. The result: greater safety and more time to enjoy the boat. These design principles are obvious, but it is surprising how often they are disregarded. I think this is why owners sometimes become disenchanted with a boat, finding that they are either a slave to it or dependent upon professional crews.

At an early stage, we discussed appearance and esthetics. Gayle and I considered duplicating the traditional Dutch lines of our previous boat—the spoon bow and high forward sheer, so pleasing to the eye—but soon chose a classic, molded, clipper bow with an exceptionally fine entry. This would give the boat a traditional look and feel (which the designer faithfully executed in other details, as well, along with her advanced underwater design). It also

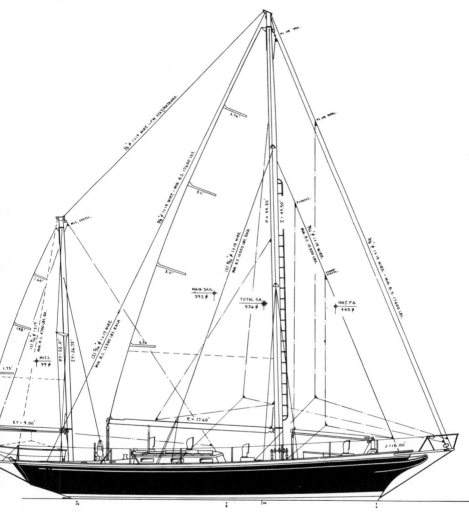

LENGTH OVER ALL .... 42'-7"
DESIGNED WATERLINE...... 32'-0"
BEAM (MAX.)............. 13'-0"
DRAFT (CBD. UP) .... 4'-3"
DRAFT (CBD. DOWN)...... 8'-3"

SAIL	MPH	WT.	FOOT	LUFF	AREA	REMARKS
MAIN SAIL		8.3	SEE	SAIL	PLAN	ROLLER REEF ; EMERG. REEF POINTS
STORM TRYSAIL		9.0	12.75	18.25	90	ROPE TACK PENNANT
STORM STAYSAIL		9.0	7.50	19.33	60	1 FT. TACK PENNANT
FORESTAYSAIL		9.0	10.67	28.00	132	
No. 2 JIB TOPSAIL		8.0	15.00	38.00	218	1 FT. TACK PEN.; 10 FT. HEAD PEN.
No. 1 JIB TOPSAIL		4.0	22.00	48.00	432	ROLLER FURLING
MIZZEN		7.5	SEE	SAIL	PLAN	1 SET REEF POINTS
MIZZEN STAYSAIL		1.5	23.00	28.00	257	
TWIN WINGS						BRITTON YACHT SYSTEMS, INC.

would create a natural line for a generous-sized pulpit, permitting a large foretriangle with its promise of good windward ability, as well as a proper place for handling ground tackle. The stern sections and transom lines were to be classic. Bulwarks would add to her sheer line and her dryness on deck, rising to 7" at the stem head.

A low-profile deckhouse for safety and seaworthiness suited our first priority—strength. I was willing to sacrifice some headroom space below, if necessary, to accomplish this, but in the final design this was not necessary. *Mischief* would have 6' 3" headroom throughout to accommodate her 6' 1" skipper. Opening ports in the 10"-high deckhouse were to be ½"-thick tempered glass.

Because we would live and cruise in the tropics, air conditioning was a temptation, but we resisted it. Instead, generous ventilation would be provided by opening ports, by seven oversized Dorade ventilators on deck, by numerous 12-volt electric fans below, and by thermal and acoustical insulation of the hull and deck from waterline to waterline. *Mischief* was to be quiet, dry, and airy below.

We decided on a shallow draft, as an owner's option, because we enjoy gunkholing shoal waters. The designed draft was 4' 3", but with full cruising stores and gear she would draw a little more. The initial keel design provided minimum wetted surface and a skeg rudder, the latter to avoid the vulnerability of a spade rudder.

At a late stage in designing, S & S made two significant changes in the keel: one, to extend its length into a traditionally long, straight run, and the other, to strengthen the skin thickness to ½" metal. Both were precautions in the event of a serious grounding in some far-off place. Anticipating an objection to the additional wetted surface, the designer reminded me that the proposed change to a long-run keel would give *Mischief* keel lines similar to the highly successful *Finisterre*. This convincing was not necessary; I approved the keel changes enthusiastically. The long keel would give *Mischief* excellent directional stability, but performance to windward was to require a centerboard, which would be solid aluminum, extending four feet below the keel line. For the centerboard pennant, ½″ hard-lay Dacron rope was chosen, rather than the usual stainless steel wire, on the assumption that the rope would be more trouble-free and longer-lasting.

Another significant design consideration was the method for carrying and handling the dinghy. I wanted to carry a rigid dinghy; one with positive built-in flotation, design stability, and lines better suited to a small outboard motor than a tender's oars. Such a small boat, in my opinion, is more versatile and reliable than a rubber boat. It certainly is a more durable lifeboat, as Dougal Robertson shows vividly in his *Survive the Savage Sea*. I selected an 8′ Perfection, a tri-hull planing design somewhat like a baby Whaler. This fiberglass dinghy is sturdy and heavy, a wet little boat under way, but quite satisfactory with a six-horsepower outboard motor. We named her *Byboot* (pronounced "bay-boot"), which is Dutch for "little boat belonging to a big boat."

For back-up and versatility, we also decided to carry a 9′ Avon Redcrest rubber inflatable dinghy. This type of craft is ideal for short excursions to docks or beach landings, or for really heavy or bulky ferrying of people, gear, and provisions.

I am prejudiced, perhaps unfairly, against stern davits, which I consider to be unseaworthy on a yacht and hazardous to a helmsman under severe conditions. Yet I did not want a rigid dinghy in the way on deck, often obstructing vision and, at the least, monopolizing deck space on a small vessel. Moreover, I wanted to be able to launch and retrieve a dinghy easily enough so one person could handle it.

This was quite a large designing order, but like many problems, having once been solved the solution seemed simple enough. My dinghy requirements promptly surfaced as the first problem to be dealt with, rather like the cart coming before the horse. After much brainstorming, some of which was highly imaginative, S & S found the answer. We would carry the dinghy on the afterdeck, lifeboat fashion, where it would be launched by the mizzen sheet tackle and mizzen boom. For this reason *Mischief*'s life-lines would terminate at the quarters. To provide an 8' space on the afterdeck without forcing the mizzen mast forward, we devised a boomkin, in effect, to lengthen the deck aft. This would have an important additional advantage of lengthening the base of the sail plan to accommodate the larger mizzen desired. Actually, in practice, it is difficult for one person to launch *Byboot;* it takes two. But the system is quite satisfactory, and her canvas-covered dinghy aft is a characteristic feature of *Mischief*'s total appearance.

Soon we turned to the intriguing challenge of developing a suitable accommodation plan. In this Gayle and I took an active part, concerning ourselves with the smallest details, for this would be our home. We wanted a "big-look" of openness and airiness below. This was to be accomplished principally by locating the boat's forward bulkhead, which partitions off the forepeak, farther forward than in a conventional layout, leaving the mast free-standing in the main cabin. Further, above the normal counter and desk heights there would be no partitions dividing the galley and navigating station from the main salon. Added to all this would be *Mischief*'s generous beam, such that the apparent cabin size as viewed from the bottom of the main hatch ladder would be an over-head area 13' wide by 11' long.

The accommodation plan had to provide ample comfort below, yet do so within dimensions which would still allow short-handed sailing. S & S considered a 32' waterline just long enough for this. Thirty-two feet is exactly what her waterline now measures, though it was not easy to hold it down to that size. The addition of "just one

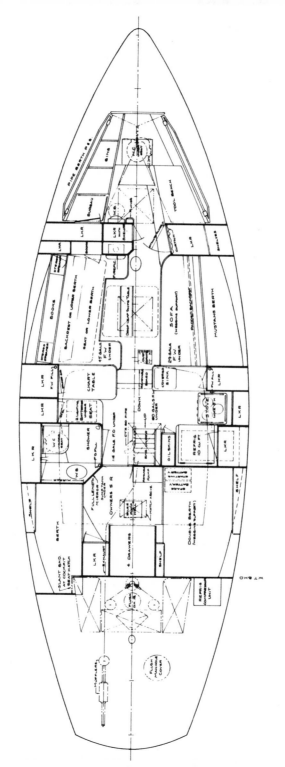

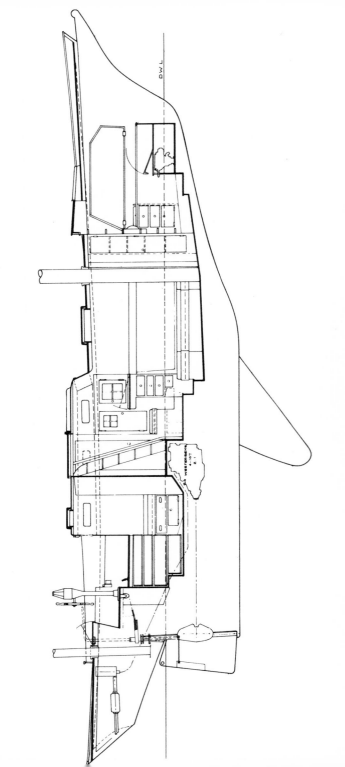

A view aft from the main salon, showing the galley to starboard and navigation desk to port. Note the signal-flag rack aft of the companionway ladder.

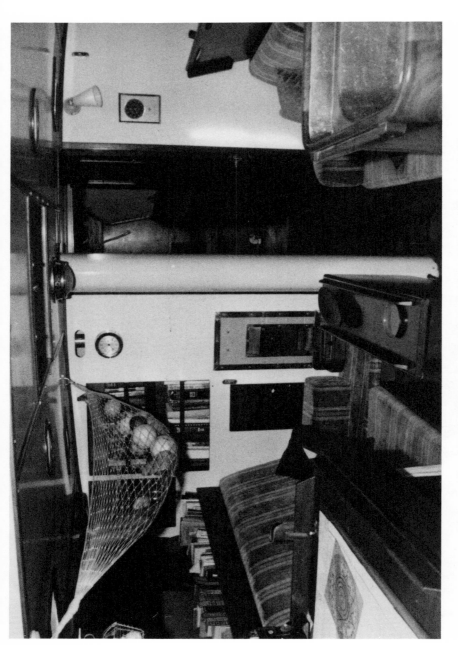

Looking forward through the main salon from the foot of the companionway ladder.

Mischief's split-level cockpit. Seat lockers at deck level around the steering position provide a walk-around bridge deck with excellent visibility. The lower seating level is deep and secure. The helmsman can keep instruments and repeaters in view without looking down.

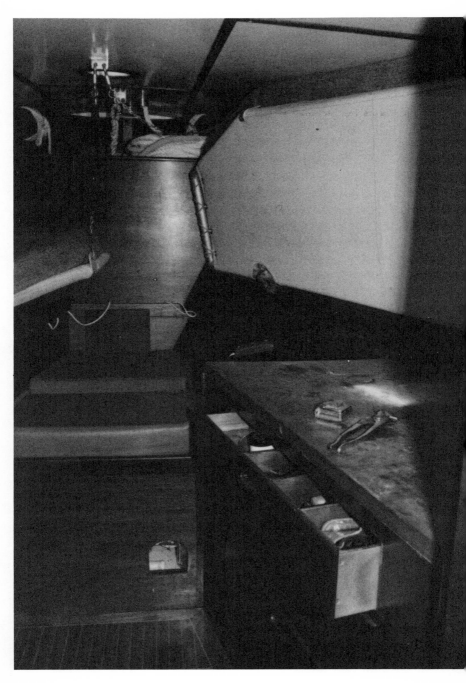

The workbench and tool drawers are on the starboard side of the forepeak, in a position under a hinged pipe-berth that folds up out of the way.

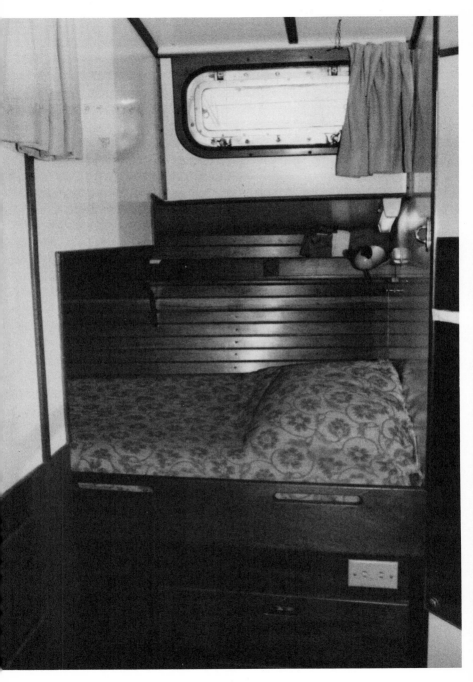

Opposite this single port bunk in the after cabin is a double berth in the same position on the starboard side.

The navigating desk, at the foot of the companionway ladder on the port side, is a model of convenience and comfort. The panel of navigation and repeater instruments is easily readable from a standing position alongside. The navigation area has an air supply from a dorade ventilator overhead, both incandescent and fluorescent lighting, 180° visibility from surrounding ports, and two outboard lockers for reference books at left and radios at right.

more foot" was more than once a plea of the designer as a solution to some accommodation problem.

Of course there were significant requirements other than comfort affecting the planning of below-deck living accommodations. Her cruising range had to be a minimum of 1,500 miles with whatever fuel tankage this would require; water capacity, at least 175 gallons. Headroom throughout had to be ample for a tall man, with bunks to suit. We wanted an after cabin for live-aboard privacy, as well as an after cockpit on deck (the room aft of that was to be taken by the dinghy). After careful calculation, we found that we would need 16 horizontal feet of bookshelves to house a ship's library suited to our reading habits, and 80 horizontal inches of hanging locker space for our year-round wardrobe requirements, plus modest additional locker space for guests. Room for radios, stereo speakers, china, linen, galley-ware, and a workbench with drawers for tools would be needed below. I also wanted an area for stowage of 800 feet of heavy anchor rodes and chain in lockers below, along with reserve tanks for stove alcohol and hot water storage (heated by engine recirculation), not to mention such things as four large 130-ampere-hour storage batteries.

We wanted the lazarette aft of the cockpit to be huge, which it is. Years later in a boatyard I emptied the lazarette and sail locker aft, so work could be done on the engine exhaust system. A workman and I were able to work together inside the lazarette. The chap from the yard asked if I had removed the bunks, evidently thinking it was an after cabin.

As the final design took shape, S & S senior designer Francis Kinney, melding our ideas with his, produced successive sets of drawings on which my alteration notes were prolific and detailed. In this creative process, discussion, not argument, was the rule. Throughout the designing stage we shared the attitude that almost anything could be done with the skills available, given the time to figure it out. No wonder *Mischief* is a happy vessel, and no wonder she turned out to be probably the "biggest 43-footer" ever seen.

The bulkhead dividing the lazarette from the after cabin was to be watertight. This would not be enough to give the boat positive flotation, but of course it would be a help in the event of serious flooding on either side. I requested this feature to meet a seldom-recognized design fallacy. In my opinion, any hinged deck opening, such as a hatch, skylight, or cockpit locker, is a dangerously weak link in the chain of watertight integrity and strength designed everywhere else into a seaworthy yacht. Even the strongest hinges, latches, and dogs are ridiculously weak compared to the rest of the deck and hull structure.

For this reason, both *Mischief*'s main hatch, located on top of the cabin trunk, and the foredeck hatch were to be sliding "scuttles," strongly boxed. But cockpit lockers present a special problem since they have to be hinged as a practical matter. Once freed from their strong latches and in an open position, it would be easy for a maverick boarding sea to tear one off and leave a gaping hole. This is why the lazarette would be a watertight compartment, with its own sump and hand-operated Henderson double-action diaphragm bilge pump. There was to be no through-hull fitting for discharge, as we wanted such fittings kept to a minimum throughout the vessel. Instead, a short length of discharge hose could be thrown overboard from this pump's fixed position.

Mischief would have a good pumping capability, some portable and some built-in. From a 45-gallon-capacity midships sump, three separate pumping systems would operate: a 56-gallon-per-minute Jabsco impeller-type pump driven off the main engine drive shaft to a through-hull discharge near the waterline; a 30 gpm hand-operated Edson diaphragm pump located under the deck just outside of the cockpit coaming and pumped with a long, double-action lever from a position within the protection of the mizzen rigging; and a 25 gpm hand-operated Henderson diaphragm pump installed under the after cabin sole. This last pump would be used primarily to empty a 15-gallon shower sump tank, but with a switch valve connecting it to an alternate intake in the main sump.

We would carry in the lazarette, accessible from deck, a 2½"-diameter portable stirrup pump with a 6'-long intake hose and a 12'-long discharge hose to be thrown overboard. Finally, we would carry a small 6 gpm portable electric utility pump which under some conditions could be a useful back-up. This would be a 1/12 hp 12-volt Jabsco "Water Puppy," mounted on an 8" × 15" plywood board for portability, with 20' of electric wire fitted with battery clamps.

The boat now carries two 50' lengths of water hose for filling tanks from a dock. In an emergency or for utility, one of these may be taken apart into two sections, 15' and 35' long, by removing a short connecting piece, leaving female fittings on both longer sections to match the intake and discharge fittings on the little motor.

When it came time for the intricate task of fitting machinery, tankage, ballast, electrical and engineering details, and laying down her lines, we deferred to the professionals. The lines were worked and reworked by Francis Kinney under the master eye of Olin Stephens. They combined the latest hydrodynamic concepts with esthetic considerations, making for a fast, seakindly, and attractive hull.

The deck plan and sail plan designing were next, with standing and running rigging specifications. In keeping with general strength requirements, her standing rigging and spars were to be oversize. Rising 49' 6" above deck, the aluminum mainmast was formed and riveted in two sections and tapered aloft. The mizzen mast was extruded. The uppers, backstay, and forestay would be 7/16″ 1 × 19 stainless wire.

To stiffen the rig under certain conditions, runners would be provided. Because runners can be a nuisance, especially when short-handed, the mast size and staying were engineered to make it unnecessary to set up runners under 25 knots of wind, unless the boat was bucking in seas. This concept was to prove quite practical for there would be times when it was a reassurance to have a windward runner set up.

Needless to say, all sheets would be handled from the cockpit. Her beamy flush deck at midships would provide generous, uncluttered space for working as well as lounging.

Mischief would have a measured sail area of 936 square feet, of which the 100 percent foretriangle of 445 square feet would form nearly half. Forty-two feet seven inches long on deck, she would be a powerful little vessel. In many combinations of sail she would fly about 1,100 square feet.

A lightweight roller-furling #1 jib topsail, or yankee, of 432 square feet would be an easy sail to handle in winds up to 20 knots, at which point this sail would be furled. A heavy 9.0-oz. club-footed staysail—the cruising man's delight—and an 8.0 oz. #2 jib topsail, together would provide a 350-square-foot hard-driving double-head rig that could be carried safely in 35 knots of wind. A heavy 60-square-foot storm jib would be carried on the staysail headstay when needed, always bagged in stops for flogging-free hoists. A 1,100-square-foot pair of 3.6-oz. nylon twin headsails, Wright Britton's "Jeni-Wings," on a single roller-furling luff wire with outrigger poles retracted on the mast would complete the foredeck sail inventory.

The 392-square-foot mainsail of 8.5-oz. cloth would be roller-reefed, when needed, with back-up reefing cringles sewn in. At sea, the 9.0-oz. storm trysail would be carried hanked onto a switch track on the mainmast, ready to be hoisted from its bag, sheets and all. Of course, the mainsail track would be reinforced where the peak of the storm trysail caused extra strain. The mizzen staysail would be 257 square feet of 1.5-oz. nylon, and the 99-foot mizzen made of heavy 7.5-oz. cloth with reef points for jiffy reefing. These sails were made by Hood in England, except the Jeni-Wings, made by Ratsey.

In the end we wound up with a 64-page, topically indexed volume of specifications and instructions for the builder, plus a large number of "S & S Type Plans" covering standard structural details and, of course, the basic design drawings for "S & S Design #2040." The designer agreed to make periodic inspections during construction at the Maas Jachtwerf, or boat yard, in Holland, but we relied mostly upon the integrity and skill of the builder. At about mid-point in construction, Gayle and I made an owners' inspection trip to Holland at the insistence of the designer.

It was a cold and raw March day when we arrived at the yard in Breskens for this purpose, on a five-day round-trip excursion flight from New York. In frequent exchanges of correspondence, names in Holland had taken on a warm character. Now we were about to meet the Dutch people who build yachts with such a tradition of quality and integrity. At the boat yard an electric sense of anticipation filled the air. Our good friend Nils Tellander of Switzerland, later to sail many miles with us on *Mischief,* drove to Breskens to join us for this occasion.

My pulse quickened as we walked from the yard offices into the covered construction shed. I was to meet my mistress for the first time! Despite her rough unpainted condition, I was awed by her beauty and size. Later I stood silently on the cement floor in front of her high cradle, facing her squarely at the bow. Alone for a moment, I reached up and patted her involuntarily, then I stroked her sharp aluminum stemhead and very nearly cut my finger.

The teak deck was laid, the metal hull had its wash-coat, and the joiner work below deck was about half-finished. Designers and builders have learned to be wary of the client/owner who does not read plans and blue-prints correctly and who may be disappointed later when seeing the real thing—thus the mid-construction meeting. I examined the boat in critical detail, liked everything I saw, made a few suggestions, and resolved some questions by the builder concerning certain custom specifications. On this occasion we cemented what had already become a cordial relationship of mutual respect between the builder and ourselves. I had expected that Frans Maas himself, no doubt from his reputation as a boat builder, would be a pipe-smoking, wise old Dutch sea-dog. I was surprised to find he was a mere 34 years of age.

In July Gayle and I returned to Holland, this time to stay. Shortly thereafter, on an overcast day in moderately rough seas and fresh winds blowing off the North Sea, for the first time *Mischief* tasted her natural element. In her sea trials in the Westerschelde River estuary, she per-formed beautifully, demonstrating an easy motion under sail or power. She was fast, powerful, and dry, with a perfectly balanced helm. The sails in their pristine new-ness set as fine as any I had ever seen, and required only minor alteration. At hand on this occasion were Roderick Stephens, Jr. of Sparkman & Stephens; Frans Maas; Dick Maddison of Hood Sails, Lymington, England; John Sum-ma from Proctor of Amsterdam, fabricator of the spars; Pieter van der Heuvel, yard foreman; and John van der Wege, yard engineer.

A dinghy paddled over; in it was Rod Stephens, ruler in hand, preparing to check *Mischief*'s waterline trim. With a builder's understandable concern, Frans Maas called for all hands to please move over onto the yacht lying alongside. No unscheduled weight is tolerated at this dramatic moment. During construction, beads of welded metal are placed at certain points on the hull at what is to be the designed waterline, and it was these that Rod measured with his stick, slowly circling the waterline. The verdict was "perfection!" This was accomplished without any inside ballast trim, for which a 500-lb. provision was allowed if needed.

At 1630 GMT in the cool afternoon sun on July 3, 1972, and in the cozy *middenhavendam* (middle harbor) of Breskens, Netherlands, an event occurred we would never forget.

"I christen this vessel *Mischief.*
May she have fair winds and safe harbors.
May she sail calmly through
Deep channels and dark waters,
With the Lord as her pilot."

Gayle's words were the beginning for us as proud owners. The precise event or even the time that marks the actual start of a new era is usually difficult to identify, and certainly this was true now. But no matter: soon enough man and boat would become as one, moving about the seas together.

Later that day, after the parchment on which Gayle's christening is recorded was signed by Frans Maas and Rod Stephens (it is now framed and mounted securely on a cabin bulkhead), very thoughtfully I made an entry on page one of Logbook One.

4

Netherlands provisioning
and shakedown

G ayle and I spent several busy weeks living aboard the
new boat at the yard in Breskens and making
occasional excursions by rented car around the province of
Zeeland, *Mischief*'s birthplace.

I cannot consider things nautical without reflecting on
this remarkable country and the reclamation of its lands
from the sea. Under pressure of necessity, partly in
ceaseless defense against the sea and partly to augment the
usable land area, the Dutch have become the world's best
drainage engineers. A century ago, the almost impossible
task of draining the water from the low-lying province of
Holland was their first large-scale project. It took 30 years
to isolate the Zuider Zee from the sea. And after the
disastrous floods of 1954, the enterprising Dutch began
another huge long-term engineering project, this one to
seal off the southwest delta area. Presently there are over
2,500 kilometers of dikes and 6,000 kilometers of canals
in this small country, and these numbers are still increasing.

One of the great modern airports of the world is
Schiphol, serving Amsterdam. Built on the bed of a
former lake which was the scene of a medieval naval

battle, the runways of Schiphol today are 13 feet below sea level. In nearly all respects Schiphol is efficient and functional, including the cultivation of land strips between runways for growing vegetable crops. Jet aircraft roaring down the runways do not seem to bother the farmer with his horse or tractor close by, tilling the land. This is typical of the Dutch: they are frugal with their limited natural resources.

Of course, traditions of the sea, so close to the Hollander, have produced skills in boat-building. This includes the building of fine yachts, a trade in which the Dutch excel. We were glad to be in such capable hands.

Each day the Maas workmen made final checks of machinery and gear or took care of small customizing jobs on the boat at our direction. "It is possible" is an endearing English expression used by the Dutch workmen in many situations. Only occasionally do they say, "It is not possible." Every evening we would manage to get the boat back into livable condition below, but the next day it would always be in disarray for one reason or another. I spent much of my time with the men, helping, learning, making many small decisions on last-minute things. Gayle assisted in much of this. She also took charge of the provisioning of foodstuffs, both staples and perishables, for our stay in the boat yard as well as for the voyage ahead.

By sampling unfamiliar brands of canned goods, one at a time, we quickly learned which were best to our taste. When it came time to stock the boat we were able to purchase selectively. We chose, for example, a case of orange juice from Israel, which to us tasted almost like fresh Florida orange juice! We found delicious green beans imported from the People's Republic of China, available at a modest price. Of course, Danish hams and bacon as well as Dutch cheeses and traditional Dutch delicacies were high on the list. Beyond a basic supply of staples, our practice was to stock up by the case when we found a particularly appealing canned product. We were fortunate that Breskens provided a wide selection of international products at reasonable prices.

People often ask if we do not tire of eating canned foods, assuming that is all you can take on a boat. The answer is that a large part of the time we eat fresh foods purchased locally as opportunity occurs. For a long voyage, however, it is prudent not to rely on fresh provisions that require constant refrigeration. Shipboard refrigeration is generally less than totally reliable. *Mischief* carries, in her main salon on the portside clear of the passageway, a 5′ net hammock swinging overhead. In this airy and colorful device we carry our main stock of fresh fruits and vegetables for all except the longest passages, when we often use two such hammocks in the cabin, port and starboard.

During these weeks there was also much for us to do in gathering, organizing, and stowing supplies and equipment which we felt were needed. We had shipped six barrels of gear over from the States and, of course, purchased additional things locally, in Rotterdam and Amsterdam. *Mischief* had a cubbyhole bin in the stock room at the yard for assembling her movable gear. Regularly, we trundled things from there to the dock for loading and stowage. I estimate that we loaded aboard about 1,800 lbs. of such stores, not including consumable provisions.

In deciding what should and should not go on a boat, I have always favored the old precept that everything should have two uses. This is not always possible, but it is an interesting game to test one's ingenuity thinking of ways to apply this rule. An example: *Mischief* carries a supply of threaded stainless steel rods of assorted diameters, with matching nuts and lock-washers; bolts of any desired length or size can be cut from these rods. From the yard I obtained a small supply of every size of nut, bolt, and screw in the material used in construction of the boat. Kept in plastic fly-boxes that fishermen use, this assortment is a gold mine to dip into for odd shipboard jobs.

For a lot of reasons, including avoidance of utter chaos, it is essential to have a stowage plan for swift retrieval of every item on board. This may be crucial on a dark and stormy night. I therefore compiled an inventory of everything on the boat from stem to stern. The resulting "stowage locator" has become a vital document on *Mischief*. It comprises a dozen typed pages of alphabetically listed items (some cross-indexed). Opposite this list are two columns: one a brief description of the item, its color, size or use; the other, its stowage location on the boat. Needless to say, this system requires that everything be put back in its proper place after use.

We shopped and browsed with delight among Rotterdam waterfront ship chandlers and discovered an especially good establishment called Navigators, in business there over 100 years. They specialize in marine instruments and navigational supplies of every description. There I bought a fine Plath sextant for half what it cost in the States; I also found special equipment such as a Walker Log, an Aldis Signal Lamp, and a number of other sometimes hard-to-find things. By courtesy of Frans Maas, purchases in most places could be charged to the yard at its customary buying discounts—a welcome opportunity. We then reimbursed the yard directly as bills came in, or in turn were billed later.

We had made three round trips through Schiphol Airport in six months, and were thankful that our daughter Martha worked for a U.S. airline and could provide us with substantial parent discounts. We made discreet use of the exceptional tax- and duty-free shopping available to transients at this airport. There we bought a new camera and a number of other things for the boat or ourselves, including a small portable Japanese tape recorder. We planned to use this for making personalized cassette recordings to mail home and for dictating our "narrative log," from which much of this book is derived.

In addition, we developed a habit of taping weather broadcasts as they were received. This let us hear a report over again to listen more closely, especially if it was in a foreign language.

This, then, was the background of the final staging and provisioning of our new boat as she lay at the dock at Breskens. She seemed more alive each day as her role as self-sufficient seagoing home steadily became more real than theoretical. At the float we witnessed at close hand the daily rhythm of the local tides. Normally the range is 17 feet; at springs, 19 feet. *Mischief,* of course, stayed where she never grounded at low water. However, it was a common sight for a yacht to pull in ahead of us and tie to the pilings on the concrete bulkhead at high water, with figure-eight lashings from a piling to the mainmast. At low water such a yacht would be aground—"on the hard" as the English call it—permitting below-waterline cleaning, repairs, or painting. In this precarious position, the boat held more or less upright by the mast lashings; people stayed aboard but they moved about with circumspection.

The tiny harbor of Breskens shelters both the Frans Maas Jachtwerf facilities and the Brussels Yacht Club, but it is dominated by the local fishing fleet. One particular weekend in early August is a traditional period of thanksgiving, Dutch style, for the bountiful catches of fish in the summer season and a time for celebration and blessing of the fleet. That weekend fishing boats were dressed with flags and the docks decorated festively. The waterfront teemed with crowds of Dutchmen in a carnival mood. Gayle and I joined in the celebrations, enjoying fine Dutch beer and music, and promenading on the docks.

In this time we became acquainted with a French couple about our age, Jacques and Lile Michèle, owners of a handsome, newly completed Maas-designed 50′ sloop named *Start.* They were spending the summer living aboard their new boat with the yard as a base while taking various short shakedown cruises. Later we came to realize that this was a sensible plan. If at all possible one should stay close to the builder's yard for quite a while, because this is the only way to be assured of prompt, informed adjustment and correction of every malfunction, however small. These inevitably occur, and once away from the yard, particularly voyaging afar as we were to do, it is often impossible to make satisfactory adjustment against builder's warranties.

For a fortnight in mid-August, everything closes down for vacation in most of Europe. The yard had a skeleton force and work on *Mischief* came almost to a stop. One day a substitute mechanic came aboard, and he was adjusting something in the electrical system of the diesel engine when it happened—sparks, a flash, an acrid smell, a lick of flame, a cloud of choking smoke! Gayle and I were aboard and nearby when this occurred. The fire was put out almost as quickly as it started, with a blast of CO_2. I know this is not as effective on electrical fires as dry chemical, but dry chemical is corrosive and it makes a mess. If CO_2 had not worked, we had a dry chemical extinguisher back-up at hand.

In seconds the nearby joiner work had been seared and the wiring in the engine area irreparably damaged. The yard fabricated and installed an entire new wiring bridle to replace the damaged factory pre-wired installation. This was an unfortunate incident and delayed our departure. While the thought occurred to me, I rejected the idea that this could in any way be a "bad omen."

Three weeks had passed since we arrived on board and *Mischief* had not left the dock! Somehow there had been no time to try her out on our own. For one reason or another, week after week, she could not go out or we could not take her out. I knew the time would come, and I must confess that I felt timid in its contemplation. Surely in the first moments when I would move her away from the crowded berth and maneuver within the small dead-end of the tidal harbor with all its obstacles, my heart would be in my throat. This beamy 43-footer seemed huge in comparison to our old 36-footer. Everything about her was so new, so clean, so shiny—and so vulnerable.

But at last the occasion for her maiden voyage arose. We had word that friends from home were in the area and would meet us in Breskens to see the new boat. The Michèles on *Start* proposed that we plan a three-day weekend cruise, *Start* escorting *Mischief* on a circular course of about 200 kilometers through nearby tidal lakes and canals. The focal point would be a visit to the ancient one-time seaport of Veere.

"La première sortie du Meez-cheef!" shouted Jacques, who spoke very little English, as he maneuvered *Start* out of our way at the Jachtwerf dock on the appointed day. *Mischief* shed her dormant feel and quietly came alive. It was August 12th; at long last we were off on a shakedown cruise.

Shortly we were clear of the small harbor. Under power we stood into the River Westerschelde in the mid-morning sunlight, made sail, and finally shut off the engine. In supreme contentment, we savored the ensuing quiet moments. *Mischief* gathered speed through the light chop of the wide river mouth, moving effortlessly; she felt solid and responsive. This was a special moment for Gayle and me: we were thrilled beyond belief! We had sailed the boat before on sea trials, but now we could claim her as our own.

Our course took us offshore into the North Sea and northeast along the coast of Zeeland, a distance of about 30 kilometers to the estuary of the Oosterschelde. Here the fishing village of Colinsplaat was faithfully rebuilt by the Dutch government in recent years at a fresh location not far from the original site, but west of a new causeway and bridge. Otherwise the local fisherman would have been landlocked by the Delta Project, which reclaimed hundreds of acres of land from the sea here.

We moored at a fishing-boat pier west of the bridge just in time to secure for a sharp squall that passed over at 1800 hours. The pier proved uncomfortable at low tide and difficult for getting on or off the boat. We went ashore, but did not venture far or long, as we were uneasy about the boats. Nevertheless, we enjoyed the sights and friendly people and had a fine Dutch dinner with local fishermen at a dockside restaurant. This was a part of Netherlands I had not seen, where women and fair-cheeked young girls wore spotless white leg-o-mutton sleeved blouses, skirts, and wooden shoes. Most of the fishermen wore boots ashore, some wore wooden shoes.

The next morning we cast off as an early sea fog drifted in. In light air we sailed and powered, losing the fog as we moved farther inland. We were on a kidney-shaped tidal lake, 30 kilometers in length. The reclaimed land has surprising fertility, and the shores almost everywhere presented a pastoral scene of fields, flowers, grass, and farmhouses. This lake extends east to a town with the catchy name of Bergen Op Zoom, but before we sailed that far, we turned southerly into the Zandkreek.

Soon this waterway ended in a cul-de-sac, and I faced my first Dutch lock in *Mischief*. I looked it over suspiciously. The near end was open; the lock appeared 50 feet wide and 300 feet long. Already it seemed filled with boats of all sizes and types, including two heavily built 200-foot steel coastal ferryboats. There was no traffic control in evidence. Every vessel was fending for itself, yet there was no disorder. *Start* had been through this sort of thing before, and she moved promptly into the lock with no apparent place to tie up. *Mischief* followed uncertainly. Friendly hands immediately took our lines and my crew hurriedly put fenders at strategic places.

The lock raised us about ten feet, cutting us off from the

sea, then disgorged its vessels into the Zandkreek, a meandering waterway that leads to Veere. In the fifteenth and sixteenth centuries, this city was a prosperous and busy seaport; now its location is 30 kilometers inland. Cut off from the sea by one of the delta dikes, Veere is undergoing economic and cultural metamorphosis. The local coat of arms shows a lion rising from the sea and there is a possibility that this area eventually may become the new Venice of Europe. The narrow cobblestone streets of Veere, the fine stone buildings of medieval architecture, the clean small lawns, flower beds and flower boxes everywhere, the freshly painted houses, and well-worn walking paths enchanted us.

On late Sunday afternoon, the third day of our cruise, we were treated to the spectacle of Dutch weekend waterway traffic along the Vlissingen Canal. Everyone seemed to have his own boat. The canal was unbelievably congested by an endless and more or less double line of vessels of all sizes and shapes returning from a weekend on the water. Some small boats without engines were tacking back and forth in the narrow waterway. We were headed in the opposite direction to this traffic and had an excellent view of the parade.

On this shakedown all went well with the boat except for two minor occurrences. Our new #2 jib caught on an exposed cotter pin everyone had overlooked and tore one panel. And Gayle had a spectacular but harmless galley fire preparing lunch while underway in the fog—a part of getting used to the peculiarities which every seagoing stove has. All told, we could not have been more content.

At 1100 hours on August 22, 1972, having completed our shakedown cruise, we prepared to slip lines and leave the Jachtwerf in Breskens. From there four of us—we took two Dutch friends—would sail across the Strait of Dover to England. Our spirits were high but also there was a certain poignancy. By leaving the yard, we were about to sever the umbilical cord that united *Mischief* with her builder. She would now claim her destiny in her natural element, the sea.

A host of yard technicians watched and helped, and soon were waving farewell to us, calling, "Dag! Dag! Goed zeilen!" (good-bye and good sailing).

5

The south coast of England

Mischief throbbed quietly as I maneuvered under power in the small harbor, then headed for the breakwater, the river, and the open sea to England. The wide river mouth near the North Sea is a conduit for a huge amount of shipping, largely to and from the port of Antwerp 50 miles upstream. Immediately we concerned ourselves with the hazards of river traffic, as well as currents and shoals in places where a small yacht seemed safest from ships.

Outside we found a fair and unseasonable northeast wind. We decided to make a straight shot across the Channel to Dover, in preference to stopping along the Belgian coast overnight. This would be a distance of about 150 miles and would take 30 hours or less. I laid a course of west northwest. *Mischief* romped along the coast under full sail with lowering sky and freshening wind. Zeebrugge, Oostende, passed on the shores of Flanders, and on the port bow we could see Dunkerque.

As afternoon shadows lengthened, I pondered the long voyage ahead for Gayle and me. We would sail beyond England, beyond Spain. I almost could not believe its surging reality. Two weeks would be all the time we could allow for cruising the south coast of England. That would be followed soon by another Channel crossing into the rough and windy Bay of Biscay to Finisterre and the Galician coast of Spain. Beyond, in dimensions of distance and time, *Mischief* would open almost unlimited horizons to us.

We took turns at the helm during the day and set watches for night, beginning at 1800 hours. As has been our practice before and since, starting at twilight the deck watch was required to wear personal safety equipment consisting of a flotation jacket or vest, a pocket-size strobe light with lanyard and whistle, a small flashlight, and a safety harness with long and short tethers. We would also don all this during the daytime in rough weather.

That first night at sea also gave us an opportunity to check other deck safety equipment. In the mizzen rigging, port and starboard, *Mischief* carried two 12'-long weighted and buoyed fiberglass man-overboard poles. The flags on them are of high-visibility orange plastic, rolled and encased in a tube lashed to the rigging. Later I installed a diagonal batten on each flag to assure that it would stand out when unfurled.

Our safety gear in the cockpit may be of interest. Our two float flags are each attached to a horseshoe life ring and a strobe light. Between the port horseshoe and its float flag I have attached a 200' length of 5/16" yellow polypropylene line. This rope is coiled carefully and is carried in the center of the horseshoe ring, contained by two light lines tied with reef knots. At a point about 10' from the end of the line I have spliced an eye into the core of the polypropylene line. One end of this line is spliced onto a D-ring of the horseshoe, the other end leads outside of everything back to the aftermost stanchion. It is secured to the base of that stanchion by a stout cord with a reef knot to the eye-splice. From there the yellow line leads forward (over the lifeline and outside) to the nearby float flag, to which the strobe light also is attached by a short lanyard.

This portside arrangement is rigged so that in an emergency the horseshoe and its coil of yellow rope may be thrown immediately. As the boat moves away, the rope pays out. A person overboard may be able to reach the floating horseshoe ring before the moving yacht reaches the end of the 200' line. If she is sailing at 6 knots, this would take about 20 seconds. If the swimmer succeeds in reaching the ring he is almost "home free." Failing that, the float flag and its tethered strobe light are dropped overboard, the reef knot at the base of the stanchion is pulled, and the whole contraption is dropped free of the vessel. Seeing the flag or its light, a swimmer is in a fair position to discover the yellow floating line and retrieve the life ring, or swim to the flag and await rescue.

The starboard horseshoe ring is tied by a 4' lanyard directly to its companion float flag and strobe light. To launch the ring one must lift it out of its holder and drop it overboard, then promptly throw over the float flag and strobe light, all of which are tied together. All reef knots securing any part of this gear from accidental launching have the pulling part tipped with red tape for quick identification of what to pull to untie the knot.

Even with thorough preparation and prompt action in a man-overboard emergency, the odds of rescue at night or in bad weather are not too good. Thus the prudent crew will concentrate on avoiding the emergency in the first place. With this in mind, we keep a pair of stainless steel lines permanently set up, flat on the deck, one port and the other starboard. Each is strongly secured to a stanchion base aft, abreast of the cockpit, and leads forward to the first stanchion in the bows. A crew member snaps his safety harness tether onto one of these in the safety of the cockpit, and then is able to move freely about the deck on either side of the mast all the way to the pulpit, securely

anchored to the vessel. Later, I rigged a supplemental 3/8"
line around the bridge deck. When crossing between the
midships hatch and the cockpit—a position from which
an emerging watch on more than one boat has suddenly
catapulted into the sea—we fasten the safety harness in
the same way.

We also carry a 25mm Very pistol and a supply of red
and white parachute flares under the lid of a cockpit
locker seat, convenient to the helmsman. The latter are
kept handy for last-minute avoidance of a ship at sea or to
light up an area in poor visibility. Another device to
reduce the risk of collision, though it assuredly does not
eliminate it, is the radar sensor. This sets off an audible
alarm when it intercepts a ship's radar beam. On dark,
stormy nights, when the watch may be partially shielded
from the windward horizon, a radar sensor could provide
the warning that saves your boat or your life.

Crossing the English Channel is never a carefree venture
for a yacht. Winds are fresh, tidal currents are strong, and
the weather is changeable. Visibility is often poor and
shipping traffic is heavy. In fact, the area may be the most
congested shipping lane in the world, due to the number
of major world ports routing traffic through this narrow
waterway. As in other similar coastal areas, commercial
shipping is strictly controlled by traffic separation lanes.
The southerly portion is for north or eastbound ships;
beyond a three-mile-wide separation zone lies the lane for
south or westbound ships.

As darkness came upon us off Calais, France, gray forms
of ships all about the horizon gradually changed to blots of
light. Identifying their navigational characteristics was
difficult. Our track cut a diagonal across the two traffic
lanes at the narrowest part of the Channel, the Strait of
Dover. First we concentrated on identifying course and
speed of vessels approaching on the port bow, monitoring
sometimes 20 ships at once as they bore down on us from
varying distances. There were so many lights around the

entire horizon that I wrote in the log that it looked like a holiday yacht-club rendezvous after dark. *Mischief* sailed smartly on starboard tack, but we dared not grant right-of-way to ourselves. I ran the engine at idle for standby if needed. Visibility was fair, and the wind was fresh.

In these circumstances perhaps we can be forgiven for being spooked by an alarming occurrence. Safely into the Separation Zone at 2200 hours, we checked our position. We were startled to discover a flashing red light about two miles ahead to port, where the chart showed none. We felt a little edgy as we considered what it could mean. Even as we studied it, the red light grew brighter, nearer, and seemed above the water level. It was a dark night, and we could not make out the outline of a ship nor other identifying lights, only the flashing red. It came still closer, at about the height of a vessel's bows. In near panic I gunned the engine and came about. The red light passed close aboard, slowly, at mast height. It was a British Coastal Patrol helicopter checking our identity!

With all hands on watch the rest of the night, we progressed without further incident through the west-bound traffic lane. At 2315 hours a bright moon came out from behind the clouds, and in an hour it illuminated the white cliffs of Dover like a horizontal streak of chalk. In the moonlight *Mischief* sailed quietly by, close inshore, on a heading for Portsmouth 100 miles to the west. The weather was clear and cool, and we had a fine coasting sail averaging 6 knots through the morning, passing Beachy Head and Selsey Bill.

By mid-afternoon we were in the harbor, berthed at Gosport Yacht Marina, a modern facility on the west bank. Across the harbor is the town of Portsmouth, home of the British Navy. A number of gray warships lay berthed, including HMS *Victory,* flagship of Admiral Lord Nelson and now a British naval shrine. This is a safe and convenient port. The upper reaches and channels provide good waters for small-boat sailing and racing. Every

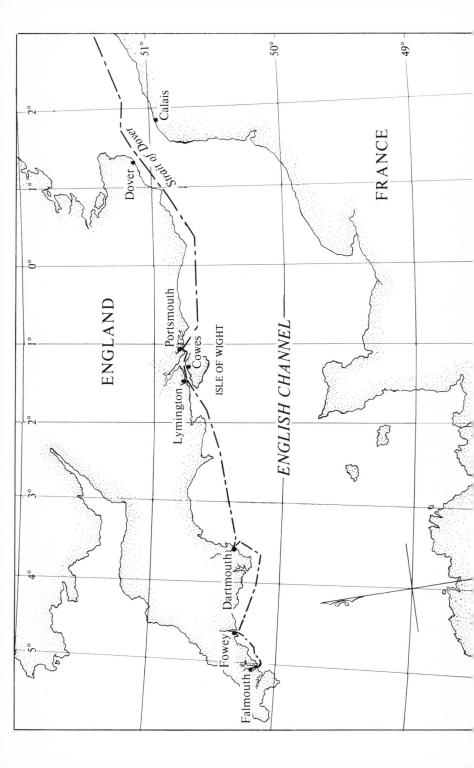

facility for yachts is to be found at Gosport and Ports-mouth, including chart-designated "hard" areas. These are hard-bottom spots that dry at low water, permitting scrubbing and inspection of one's boat, as we had seen before in Breskens. Despite its being so commonplace, a yacht "drying on the hard" always was a startling sight to us.

Along the length of the south coast the tidal range tends to be higher in the eastern and western thirds than in the middle third. The former average 20 feet or more in springs, 16-plus in neaps. Average tidal range in the middle third is 10 to 13 feet. Individual harbors and rivers vary considerably from one another, and the careful navigator makes due allowance. Not far away, across the Channel in the vicinity of Mont St. Michel, tides are 45 feet high.

We were endlessly fascinated by the sights and situations encountered at low water: the omnipresent stranded dinghy—on occasion our own—and the long muddy stretch to the nearest water; some boats with suitable bottoms sitting upright in a seabed that looked as solid as a brick floor, their owners seemingly oblivious to their strange (to us) circumstance; other boats lying askew like wounded birds on the bottom. All life ashore and afloat was geared to the rhythm of the daily tides. We were quick to learn that the sailing auxiliary sometimes "can't get there from here," as the old Down East saying goes, against a foul tide.

After a short layover in Gosport, we sailed on an ebb tide, soon finding the unseasonable northeast breeze holding fair to our intended course. It was late August, and *Mischief* voyaged in cool sunny days. These were said to be the first sunny days of the season, but no doubt that was an exaggeration. With a light reaching breeze we carried the big yankee and for a while the red mizzen staysail. Passing yachts would alter course occasionally to come have a look at us, and we would exchange greetings. We were now feeling much more at home with the new boat, and prolonged the short sail to Cowes for the sheer joy of it.

The Isle of Wight is a 100-square-mile offshore island protecting the Solent and the Spithead and their mainland harbors. The island is bold with rocky headlands and rolling green hills. At Cowes is a world-famous yachting center and the headquarters of the Royal Yacht Squadron. Under power with mainsail only, flying the New York Yacht Club burgee, *Mischief* inched around the inner harbor to view the sights and seek a berth. Nearby at her mooring was *Morning Cloud,* former British Prime Minister Ted Heath's racing yacht destined to go down with loss of life two years later in a violent August gale not far from where we recently had sailed.

For a fortnight the precious northeast breeze held, favoring our westerly progress. To the west of us, 225 miles away in the Scilly Islands, late-season British yachtsmen were waiting impatiently for the return of normal westerlies on which to reach homeward from their sailing holidays. By the last week of August, mindful of advice to clear the British Isles soon after September 1, if southbound, or risk being weathered in for the winter, we curtailed our meandering in this attractive cruising area and made our plans more purposefully. Lymington was our next destination, across the Solent about 20 miles from Cowes.

Off the mouth of the River Lyme are large mud flats, dry at low water. On the starboard side of the entrance, barely into the deeper water, the Royal Lymington Yacht Club maintains an unusual offshore facility: a staging platform and starting box for Race Committee officials. As we entered, we dropped sails and powered cautiously a mile or so upriver, then berthed at a large modern marina in an area where the river had been dredged extensively.

Looking back toward the river mouth at high water, the narrow winding channel was lost in an immense spread of water across the flats, while at low water the exposed channel looked like a winding trickle about to dry completely. There were a large number of sailing boats of every size and type in the mud along the river flats, anchored or moored along the narrow, winding river channel, and at the marina. At low water boats were strewn about in various positions of stranding creating the appearance of some recent sea disaster. Transit in the channel could be difficult for a newcomer, particularly with the hourly arrival and departure of the broad-beamed Yarmouth ferry.

In Lymington we enjoyed adapting ourselves to local British customs. We lunched in a cozy pub, shopped, and walked around town sightseeing. Along the waterfront, Lymington's narrow streets were reminiscent of Marblehead, or vice versa. A taxi excursion inland gave us a chance to see some of the countryside which lies within commuting distance of "the city," to travel to Salisbury Cathedral, and to view the enthralling mysteries of ancient Stonehenge.

This port also is the home of Brookes & Gatehouse, supplier of *Mischief*'s electronic equipment, and of Hood Sails, her sailmaker. In two days we had all instruments rechecked and calibrated by Brookes & Gatehouse engineers, including Major Richard Gatehouse himself. During an afternoon sail in the Solent with Hood Sails' local manager aboard, we checked the fit of all sails, this time after some reasonable use. Also *Mischief* had her first chance to fly her huge blue-white-and-yellow-striped Jeni-Wings in a test run.

One afternoon at 1500 hours a Brookes & Gatehouse engineer came aboard to supervise a timed run down and back up the river to calibrate the speed indicator. Tide was at half ebb, and yachts were powering back to their berths. As other small boats without engines tacked back and forth endlessly across the channel, I began to sense the ordeal that lay ahead. At 1530, with *Mischief* uneasily in mid-stream, the Yarmouth ferry left the town dock upstream and swooped down the middle of the channel at flank speed. At that moment the engineer instructed me from below to "proceed downstream at as high a speed as you can safely maintain—at least 5 knots." Quite an assignment! We called out the numbers of the channel markers on the port hand and the time by stopwatch when abeam of each. The engineer had these distances exactly measured for timed runs. At the mouth of the river we turned and duplicated the run back upstream. We repeated the whole procedure twice, getting a little more gray hair each time.

On the second downstream leg, a returning Lymington-Yarmouth ferry arrived. She swept traffic to both sides, including *Mischief*. A pair of tacking sailboats forced me to turn to port and pass the ferry on the wrong side, without benefit of horn signal. I was reminded of this by a number of good-natured voices from the upper deck of the ferry. Eventually we finished the calibration. Once back securely in our slip at the marina we felt shaken enough to warrant an earlier Happy Hour than usual.

That same day, August 30, we found a radiogram waiting for us from the States, obviously an urgent message. It was from our sailing friend, Dr. Robert Simpson, then Director of the National Hurricane Center at Miami. It read in part, "Tropical hurricane Betsy approaching Azores. Course uncertain next 48 hours. Advise caution and further information before leaving England to Bay of Biscay." This was sobering information, and uneasily we kept it in the back of our minds.

On a hazy day *Mischief* sailed from Lymington out the Solent and through the Eye of the Needle westbound for Dartmouth, 92 miles along the coast. Our track was close inshore much of the time, affording a marvelous opportunity for sightseeing of the shoreline. The land stands bold along the south shore of England, and almost everywhere it has the cultivated beauty of neat, green, rolling hills, lovely to view from the sea. Half a dozen major rivers and many smaller ones flow into the sea from interior highlands. Many form deep cuts in the land with narrow fjord-like entrances, like the River Dart; others empty into a vast expanse of tidal flats, like the River Lyme. Along most portions of the south coast a large variety of harbors, rivers, and coves await the cruising yachtsman. Away from the big cities there is a quality of the past that intrigues visitors. Everywhere one feels the secure dignity that comes from a long recorded history.

In late afternoon we sighted Dartmouth Light. (The name Dartmouth, of course, is derived from the River Dart.) From the sea the approach is dramatic. Entering from the south one sees the craggy Mewstone Rock (115 feet high) close inshore, east of the entrance. Farther east a series of rocks jut out from the shore, the largest being East Blackstone Rock. On either side of the opening are high bluffs topped with rolling fields and wooded areas, and to the west lies West Blackstone Rock. Guarding the river mouth are Dartmouth Castle, built in 1388, and Battery Point to port, with Kingswear Castle to starboard. In times of danger long ago a chain was put across the entrance; during World War II this old-fashioned method was used to block marauding U-boats.

Sailing between the two headlands, at times carrying when the wind was blocked, *Mischief* followed the center of the river, which curves sharply to the west. Beyond this turn the natural harbor is protected from the wind and sea in all weather. Here is the home of Dartmouth Academy, the Annapolis of the British Navy, located on steep hills above the west bank. An ancient square-rigger belonging to the naval school rides in the harbor. We berthed *Mischief* at Dart Marina in evening twilight, as the lights and shadows of the town cascaded over the steep hillsides bordering the river like a picture in a storybook.

A few days in Dartmouth were not enough to savor this

beautiful place, but with an eye on the fall weather, we had to push on. We had work done on the anchor windlass, explored the harbor with the dinghy, poked around a bit ashore, then on September 2 *Mischief*'s lines were cleared after an early breakfast. The BBC weather forecast for this area was easterly winds Force 4 to 5, locally 6, fair weather and good visibility. We made sail in the harbor, rolled a reef in the main, and sailed out the narrow river with a fair wind. It is remarkable how quickly one sometimes develops an attachment for a certain place. Dartmouth was such a port.

Falmouth, the most westerly natural deep-water harbor on the south coast, was our last English port before heading south. We used an absent yacht's home mooring some distance from the club landing, and launched *Byboot* for the first time. Previously we had been using the inflatable Avon, so easy to launch and retrieve and comfortable to bang around beaches and docks. Five of us now on *Mischief,* dressed in our best shore clothes for dinner at the yacht club, carefully boarded *Byboot.* There was an alarming reduction in freeboard, but the water was calm. We all agreed to sit very quietly and avoid the need for two long trips ashore in the dinghy. Almost immediately a small wake from a passing launch swamped us, and five people rose as one to keep their bottoms dry, causing more water to slosh aboard. With howls of laughter and with resignation to our plight, we crept to the safety of the club boat ramp. A "poor show," as the British call such things, although sailors ashore, of course, were too polite to comment.

Nor was that the end of it. Five hours later, after dinner, drinks, and exchanging of sea stories with hospitable fellow sailors, the club closed down to a small group of hangers-on, including ourselves. We left with best wishes from our British friends for fair winds and safe harbors and threaded our way carefully down the three stories of winding wooden steps, only to find *Byboot* high and dry on a mucky grass bottom a quarter-mile, it seemed, from the water. From up top we were unable to lift the heavy little boat onto the ramp to carry it back to the water. Who, then, would walk through the grassy muck in the dark to help lift her stern? And should good shore shoes be sacrificed, or should bare feet be used? One of our crew fearlessly volunteered, and with the help of friends from the bar we lifted the boat and carried her back to the water. Another poor show.

The next day was September 4, three days past the time I had earlier hoped to be on our way. We busily engaged in ship's chores, checked equipment, shopped for provisions ashore, and did a little sightseeing—all in two days. *Byboot* was busy in taxi service.

We monitored the regular BBC weather broadcasts, now with special concern for the progress and course of Hurricane Betsy. I telephoned the local meteorological office, a highly efficient government facility, and picked up helpful information to supplement the regular BBC "shipping weather synopsis and forecast," called in short form the "shipping forecast." This service, in my experience, is unique for its scope and reliability. The government-owned British Broadcasting Corporation broadcasts four times daily on 200 kHz and VHF, giving a general synopsis of the weather, weather data from selected coastal stations, and a 24-hour forecast of wind, weather, and visibility by sea sectors.

Of course, at that time our special interest was in the offshore areas designated as Plymouth, Sole, Finisterre, and Biscay. Having missed the traditional September 1 "leave-or-else" date, gales became a problem, and I had to face the music—whether to push on south, or lie safely in harbor until a promising forecast arose. If we stayed in safe harbor much longer, we risked being weathered in by a series of gales with too little space in between to get safely south. In short, there was a good chance we would winter involuntarily in England.

Mischief and crew were readied for an uncertain departure date. Meanwhile the hurricane turned northerly, increasing the threat to us even in Falmouth Harbor. Then, within 12 hours, it stalled and degenerated. Among my companions there was a mixed feeling of interest and apprehension for the sea voyage ahead. As always in circumstances involving some risk, Gayle and I talked things over in private and agreed on what to do. The BBC evening forecast was favorable, and we decided to go.

In the peaceful early evening of September 5, *Mischief* sailed out of the port of Falmouth, after a hot dinner for all hands in harbor. Under full sail in a light easterly breeze, she reached on the port tack. The sea voyage to Spain lay ahead across the Bay of Biscay. We would give this stormy area a wide berth in a bending track, as the season of fall gales was predictably near. At 2030 hours we took our offing from Lizard Light, bound for Cape Finisterre, 500 miles to the south.

6

Bay of Biscay gales

Sailing directions and local information had warned us about the rough and windy weather typically encountered during fall months in the Bay of Biscay. As the season develops, a succession of westerly gales tends to move across this latitude, piling turbulent water into the deep bay.

The 500 or so miles from Falmouth to Cape Finisterre should have taken us about 84 hours to sail, or three and a half days, assuming an average speed of 6 knots. But sailing under adverse conditions, it eventually required six days and nights—146 hours elapsed time. This first test of the new boat and her crew in heavy offshore going broke a few pieces of gear, but I considered these normal shakedown failures. Most importantly, it proved the boat to be seakindly and rugged. The slow passage, I felt, in no way reflected adversely on the boat; for a total of 20 hours, at separate times, we were virtually hove-to on an offshore tack.

We crossed the channel at its wide westerly entrance without incident. I doubled the watch under the circumstances, and we all agreed to four-hour tricks. This later proved to be a hardship when the weather worsened. At times the watch bill, posted on the galley bulkhead, was ignored under the press of conditions, especially in view of the frequent sail changes we undertook. After the first day, we generally kept two-hour watches.

A few hours out of Falmouth the wind fell light and hauled into the south. It was slow going on the port tack with our sails strapped in and the engine at cruising rpm. In this trim *Mischief* lacked the power to breast the lumpy seas, so we eased sheets to foot better and tacked our way through the first night and most of the next day. I favored the port tack as it lee-bowed the adverse easterly-flowing current we encountered.

It was not until late afternoon on the first day, almost 24 hours underway, that we rounded formidable Ushant Light, about two miles off the coast of France. Visibility at that time was limited; we could hear the diaphone but could not see the light. We gauged our distance off by successive bearings on the diaphone, which sounded two blasts every two minutes. We factored in our distance run as one leg of a triangle, and took hand-compass bearings on the sound. Needless to say, this was imprecise at best, but it did provide a sense of relief that we were rounding the dangerous shore with room to spare. Once clear of this northwest corner of France and its outlying dangers, we squared away to a southwesterly heading into the night.

The seas were lumpy and confused, typical of the area around any continental cape. The wind was light and variable, the sky overcast, the barometer falling. The going continued to be slow and a little frustrating. During the first 24 hours we covered 120 miles at an average speed of 5.0 knots, but most of this distance was gained the first night.

Navigating beyond Ushant we used, for one line of position, a Consolan station in Southern France designated "Ploneis." We crossed this line with coastal radio beacons where possible. (Weather permitted no celestial work until we finally sighted the coast of Spain in the sunlight.) A careful record of our DR track was kept, but of course I was aware that the need for frequent tacks would hurt our accuracy over a period of time. This later proved to be the case.

On the second day out, September 7, the morning BBC weather report was logged "light and variable, becoming west 4" in the Biscay and Finisterre areas. We made a number of experimental sail changes—too many according to the crew, too few according to the skipper. The going was still slow because of turbulent sea conditions and light air. We averaged about 3 knots until afternoon, when we had a few good hours using a double-head rig with the #2 jib top and staysail. The wind backed from WSW to SW to SSW and forced us to tack in order to accomplish some westing. The second 24 hours we made good only 85 miles for an average speed of 3.5 knots.

September 8 was the day we faced our first full gale. The sky that morning was overcast, a lead-gray color, and the barometer fell gradually most of the day. The wind freshened and hauled to WSW. *Mischief* began to pick up speed, but I did not like the look of the sky and the falling barometer. The midday BBC weather broadcast confirmed my suspicions: "gale warnings, Force 7, westerly, north Finisterre." I must admit that with a new boat, whose performance characteristics had not yet become second nature to me, and in unfamiliar and inhospitable waters, this news sent a chill up my spine.

Among *Mischief*'s equipment at the navigating desk is a "Heavy Weather Check List" in laminated plastic, reproduced here. Fatigue or anxiety, or just plain activity, can interfere with clear thinking—hence this convenient safeguard. We went through the list crossing out the numbers with a grease pencil as we awaited the gale. There is nothing strikingly original about the content of the list, as any competent seaman will recognize. But it can be an invaluable aid for boathands as yet unfamiliar with the routine.

HEAVY WEATHER CHECK LIST

Below

1. Close and dog all ports and forward hatch.
2. Secure loose gear below.
3. Empty bilge and sump.
4. Stuff pillow into china locker.

Topside

5. Secure all movable deck gear with extra lashings.
6. Lower and stow roller-furling headsails.
7. Hank storm jib onto forestay, ready to hoist, lashed down with sheets rigged aft.
8. Reef mainsail before furling.
9. Remove any ventilators on deck and install storm-caps.
10. Check availability of storm trysail on deck, slides secured in switch track, sail in bag ready to hoist.
11. Test-run main engine.
12. Haul in taffrail log and stow.
13. Set up port and starboard running backstays.
14. Lash life-ring buoys with reef knots.
15. Rig heavy warp on afterdeck for dragging if necessary.

General

16. Flotation gear for all hands. Use wet suits when available.
17. All hands carry yacht's standard personal safety equipment.
18. Navigator fix position.
19. Serve a hearty meal (optional).
20. Secure the galley.
21. Review this check list with the Skipper.

Please, once the boat is secured no ports or hatches are to be cocked open without the Skipper's approval. No smoking below while dogged down, as fresh air is a scarce blessing.

One of the items on the list is the rigging of a warp for dragging, if necessary, to slow the vessel through steep seas. I always rig such a line before an offshore passage of any length. For this purpose I use a 280' spare anchor rode of ¾" nylon, leaving it coiled on deck at the stern quarter. The bitter end at the bottom is fastened to a cleat on one side, and the bitter end at the top (led aft outside everything) is similarly fastened on the other side. To use it, one need only untie two light restraining lines and cast the entire coil overboard. When it fetches up, it forms a 140'-long bight. I have known yachtsmen who met this same need by carrying an old automobile tire securely fastened to a long rope and then trailed.

In the now-promised gale I did not want to be blown into the Bay of Biscay lying in our lee, east of us. We continued tacking as before to gain westerly sea room, generally without regard to our intended course toward Finisterre, and we picked up some distance sailing briskly. By 1530 hours the wind was Force 7, 30 knots out of the west. We shortened sail while it could still be accomplished with reasonable comfort and safety, handing the #2 jib and reefing the main. We continued sailing as before, and by early evening it was blowing 40 to 45 knots, a strong gale. Seas were building up to awesome heights in a confused pattern.

We rolled a deeper reef in the main, and finally took it down to slow the boat, and raised the mizzen. In this trim, with mizzen and staysail sheeted well in, and with the engine at slow rpm, we lay virtually hove-to on an offshore heading all night. The vessel was easy and comfortable, the engine driving us at an average speed of about 2 knots, 20° off the wind. The gale lasted eight hours, long enough for the sound in itself—the ceaseless roar of the ocean and whine of wind in the rigging—to be tiring. Despite the storm, life on board continued its routine. Hot meals—dinner and breakfast—were on time.

Several times during the night we encountered fleets of fishing vessels, sometimes numbering five or six, hove-to in company with each other. We attempted to signal these boats without success. They puzzled us at first because, even after we decided they were fishing boats, we were not sure whether they were hove-to or were dragging nets slowly. I now feel quite sure that they were hove-to. They did not appear to maintain proper lookouts—a hazard to a yacht herself lying hove-to in bad weather. More than once we had to sail carefully among these vessels as they lay strewn across our intended track.

Toward dawn the gale abated somewhat, and *Mischief* required more sail to make progress through the heavy seas. Unless it is absolutely necessary, we try to avoid sail changes at night. We therefore often shorten down at evening twilight, even though it may mean less distance covered during the night. A cockpit conference concluded that in this case we should put up the storm trysail for more drive in the expected heavy going as we turned southwesterly again. This is an easy sail for us to break out because it is always carried hanked on to a switch-track on the mainmast, bagged with its sheets tied on and lashed in position at the foot of the mast. *Mischief* welcomed the additional driving power. By early afternoon we changed to reefed main and #2 jib top with staysail. I wanted to make some distance southwesterly to swing below the track of the westerly gales that were now marching seasonably from the Azores toward northern Europe.

In a few hours we were again burdened with a howling wind. With all hands on deck we shortened sail to spitfire jib and storm trysail, to ride along with a west-southwest wind at Force 8, 35 to 40 knots.

During the 24 hours ending at 1800 on the third day, September 8, we made good only 61 miles. At 2000 hours on September 9 my entry in the ship's log read "Southwesterly gale, Force 8. Steering 165°. Speed 6.1. Served hot sit-down meal in cabin to all except Hans on schedule.

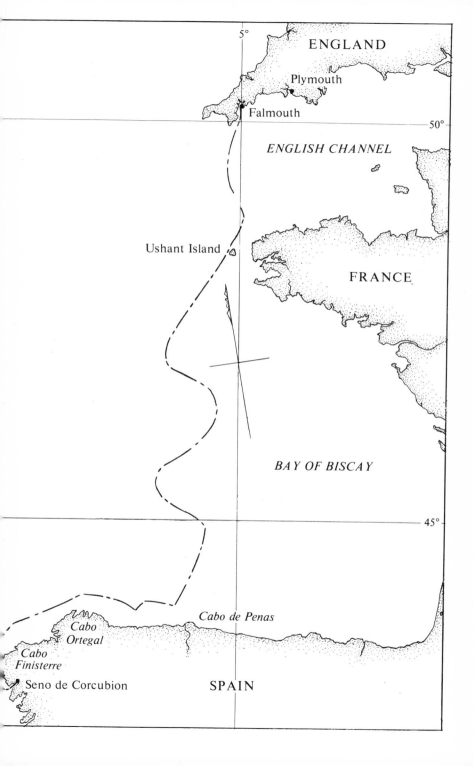

Gimballed table. Stereo music. Comparative comfort below. *Mischief* is proving very seakindly. Steering across the seas, which are quite steep and confused, at maximum safe speed." By midnight the gale moderated and we had a great sail more or less on course.

These periods of howling winds and crashing seas revealed a new dimension of *Mischief*'s comfort—her insulated hull and deck. With 1″-thick, hard-bat, inert insulation extending from waterline to waterline, she provides both acoustic and thermal protection. The quiet and relaxed atmosphere below has prompted a descending watch on countless occasions to remark on the striking difference in atmosphere between the storm above and the calm below.

During the early morning hours of the fifth day, September 10, *Mischief* romped through lumpy seas, averaging 4 to 5 knots on course. She sailed comfortably and without strain; the local wind had shifted to NNE. I calculated that land was nearby, and tried without success to reach one of several radio beacons in the vicinity of Finisterre. With the wind shift, visibility gradually improved. We had covered a little over 400 miles at sea, and the coast should have been near.

Then at 0920 the deck watch shouted an electrifying "land ho!" and all hands save one piled out on deck excitedly. The other called jubilantly from a bed of suffering, "we are saved!" This all-too-heartfelt cry was destined to become a good-natured byword on the vessel as we later recalled the discomfort of this passage.

Through the clearing weather to the south, tiers of high mountains rising 3,000 feet out of the sea appeared in line, bearing west southwest. Our course was changed to close obliquely with the land, which at the time we could not identify. Soon the sun came out and we piled on sail with exuberance. Our DR position at the time of the landfall was 44° 23′ N by 8° 17′ W, a calculation which placed us 98 miles north northeast of Cape Finisterre Light.

Judging from the extent of the land we could see to the west, this DR position appeared to be in considerable error. I continued to work with the radio direction finder, and at 1025 hours I obtained a fix, using the Cabo de Peñas radio beacon and the Lugo Consolan station in northern Spain. Our actual position was 100 miles east southeast of the DR, at 43° 49′ N by 6° 12′ W. This was confirmed when we measured 65 fathoms of depth as we sailed onto soundings. The westerly gales had forced us far back into the Bay of Biscay. Under the circumstances it was well I had chosen to face the wind and sea with some way on, rather than heave-to and drift even farther, perhaps critically, toward the easterly lee shore.

In my experience the landfall itself, hazardous and exciting though it may be, is almost invariably anticlimactic. Approaching from the sea, one often gets the entirely false feeling that arrival is imminent. We actually had another 31 hours to go before the hook would be down and *Mischief* safely tucked in the cove behind Finisterre. Nonetheless, most of us changed enthusiastically to clean warm-weather clothes and dressed like Sunday-afternoon sailors. We enjoyed a day of pleasant sailing along the scenic mountainous coast toward the Cape. As of 1700 hours the log read: "A great romping sunlit sail along the Spanish coast. Broad reaching all afternoon. Speed 6 to 7."

I reflected that in the days before this landfall we had faced two Force 8 gales and our new ship had proved easily equal to them. All she asked was to be properly canvassed. This part of the voyage had united the skipper, the crew, and the ship, as the rhythm of watch-keeping pervaded all else.

Cape Finisterre is a bold headland with deep water close to the rocky shoreline. North and southbound shipping cut this corner to save time and distance. High seas traffic in this area is controlled by traffic separation lanes, as in the English Channel. Here, the easterly lane is for northbound ships. My plan was to hug the coastline on a course that would keep us safely inshore of the shipping lane; we would sail between the northbound lane and the coast. As we bore away southwesterly and then south southwesterly, the north northeasterly breeze hauled astern and almost died. In the evening twilight we took successive bearings on Cabo de Bares, Cabo Ortegal and Punta Candelaria, as we prepared to round the large headland during the night and cover the remaining 90 miles.

At 2100 hours we furled the big roller-furling yankee, which was being blanketed by the main; an hour later, about a mile offshore, we handed the main, started the engine, put up the staysail, and proceeded motoring with staysail and mizzen in a light breeze. At 2310 hours the engine stopped suddenly. I hit the starter button and the engine started immediately, but as I put it back into gear, it stalled. We discovered that a line was caught in the propeller. Now we were without engine, almost without wind, and disturbingly close to the rocky shore. In these circumstances Gayle made an obvious but, at such times, an often-overlooked observation: "Well, don't forget that this is a *sailing* boat!"

All hands turned out to put up sail, and we ghosted the rest of the night. We had to squeeze between the rocky shore on the port hand and northbound ships, from which we could not maneuver, to starboard. But the night passed without further incident as we followed the procession of coastal navigation lights toward Finisterre.

Fortunately visibility was good, for the chart of this area (N.O. 37035) states as a caution: "The coast should be given a wide berth at night or in thick weather. Many of the lights are placed so high that they are frequently obscured by fog or mist. When the position of a vessel is not absolutely certain, continuous soundings should be taken and a course maintained through depths greater than 70 fathoms."

Throughout the next morning the wind was still light.

With the help of a late afternoon southeasterly breeze coming around the Cape, we covered the 75 miles after the propeller fouled in 17 hours, at an average speed of 4.4 knots. *Mischief* was to display an excellent light-air ability on countless occasions.

Rounding Cape Finisterre in evening twilight, we tacked with the big yankee in a soft breeze into Seño de Corcubion toward a cove in back of the cape. We had selected this on the chart and then by eye as a cozy and accessible anchorage. There our vessel stopped for the first time in six days. We dropped our hook off a steep sandy beach tucked into the northwest corner near a small fishing village.

It was hard to believe that *Mischief* had actually stopped. Spirits were high and we declared a Happy Hour, which was all the more welcome because of our rule of abstinence underway. Soon the lights of the nearby village twinkled on. Cape Finisterre Light under a starry sky looked quite different to us, as we viewed it from the rear. We were ready to enjoy the beautiful Galician coast. Beyond, the Mediterranean Sea beckoned.

7

The Galician coast and Lisbon

In the procession of tiring watches from England, we had all agreed that once in port we would spend the entire first day sleeping. The second day would be devoted to cleaning up the boat and then ourselves. Only then would we venture ashore. But by noon of the first day, at anchor in peaceful Seño de Corcubion, all this had been accomplished, and soon we were eager to move on to a totally different environment—the Galician coast of Spain.

The region of Galicia comprises the northwest corner of the Iberian Peninsula. In this area of 50 square miles there are literally hundreds of miles of broken shoreline. Local fishing fleets are in evidence in nearly every small harbor. It is a region of heavy rainfall but August and September are normally the dry season. We enjoyed this climate at its best, a relief from the heavy rains we had encountered farther north at sea.

To a cruising yacht the glory of Galicia is its chain of rias, or fjord-like indentations, that reach inland along the length of the west coast from Cape Finisterre south to Bayona. Most of the time these waters are calm, sheltered from the harsh Atlantic by offshore islands and hills, but strong northeast winds sometimes pour down the narrow bays, making it difficult for a sailboat to work inland. The rias cut their way into what for centuries was considered *finis terrae*—land's end—because west of it lay only the open ocean. There are five major rias, each extending 10 to 20 miles into the hilly coastline. Relatively few yachts visit this area; it is perhaps most familiar to yachtsmen passing from northern Europe to the Mediterranean, as we were, or returning.

During our cruise of the Spanish coast, we learned to expect that in Spain yacht clubs in most cases were simply social clubs or private waterfront restaurants. Often no boating activity would be in evidence, and no facilities were available for yachts. Exceptions to this generalization were rare. Therefore, a visiting yacht was well advised to avoid mistaking a *club nautico* in a strange harbor for an inviting, or even usable, berth.

One morning, as we turned into the mouth of the Ria de Vigo on our way to Bayona, the wind died completely. After experimenting a bit with the sails unsuccessfully, and observing no current to help, we finally gave up, dropped the sails, and started the motor. The engine, normally a paragon of reliability, would not fire, nor would it respond to the skipper's ministrations. With sails back up and drooping, we tried to get out to sea, but had no steerage. The bay sounded at 150′—too deep for anchoring. The south bank was menacing; a perceptible drift to starboard began to carry us toward the rocks.

Awkwardly, we tried to paddle the boat using dinghy oars. Then we launched *Byboot,* lashed it fore and aft with fenders and stretched tight breast lines and spring lines hard on the port quarter of *Mischief,* fired up the little six-horsepower outboard motor, and at once had a creditable tugboat. It always is a surprise to me what a small amount of energy is required to move a fairly heavy sailboat through calm water, once inertia is overcome. Towing is the least effective method because energy is absorbed in the towing line. It is best to push if there is a way to do so,

Chores like painting the deckhouse can wait when a breeze comes up.

Mischief's *uncluttered working foredeck and pulpit. In the foreground at the stemhead is the furling drum for the twin Jeni-Wings.*

The rigid 8' tri-hulled dinghy is carried lifeboat style on the afterdeck and is launched by tackle from a slide under the mizzen boom.

Mischief *sails to windward in light air under main, mizzen, and lightweight Yankee.*

This view illustrates **Mischief***'s broad beam and full bilge lines.*

A view aft from the spreaders as **Mischief** *slides along in a light breeze, leaving a trail of bubbles rather than a quarter wave.*

Above: *Breakfast for three served on the removable mahogany table that locks onto two stainless steel fittings mounted on the after cabin bulkhead with short legs resting on the mainsheet trimming track. The porthole pass-through is a much-used convenience.*

Below: *At anchor after our transatlantic passage.*

Mischief *under full sail.*

and any yacht with a dinghy and outboard has such a way.

Unfortunately we were low on gasoline for the outboard and decided to save some for last-ditch uses. Running the little boat intermittently, we spent six hours making the last three miles to Bayona in a dead calm, ghosted into the harbor at sundown, and again anchored off a "yacht club," in this case a proper one.

We relaxed at Bayona, stocked up on fresh provisions, enjoyed the shore facilities of the *club nautico,* and waited for a threatening weather pattern to disperse. It was then September 20. If we were to get around Cabo St. Vincent to Gibraltar and on to the Balearic Islands by September 30, as planned, we needed to push ahead to make the 1,000-mile trip comfortably, with stopovers, in ten days. The reason for such scheduling was that I had to return to Miami on business for two weeks beginning October 1. During this unwelcome interlude, I planned to leave *Mischief* safely berthed in Palma de Mallorca. From Mallorca we would sail leisurely about 1,100 miles across the Mediterranean during late October and November to winter in Greece. In November the eastern Med would be marginally safe. Soon after, winter storms, locally called *meltemi,* would begin to sweep down out of the Balkans.

Mid-morning on September 21 we left Bayona, after taking an hour to clear a fouled anchor caught on a heavy mooring chain on the bottom. I have seen this happen many times in the Mediterranean with other yachts and occasionally with *Mischief;* it is unavoidable when so many small harbors have heavy chains or cables on the bottom in positions known only to local people.

By noon we were clear of Ria de Vigo, leaving behind us the Galician coast of Spain. Our course was southerly along the coast of Portugal. Wind was north northeast at 20 knots, and *Mischief* sailed comfortably at 5 knots under shortened canvas with staysail, trysail, and mizzen. Before long the wind moderated and died. We continued under sail and power through the first night, enjoying coastal

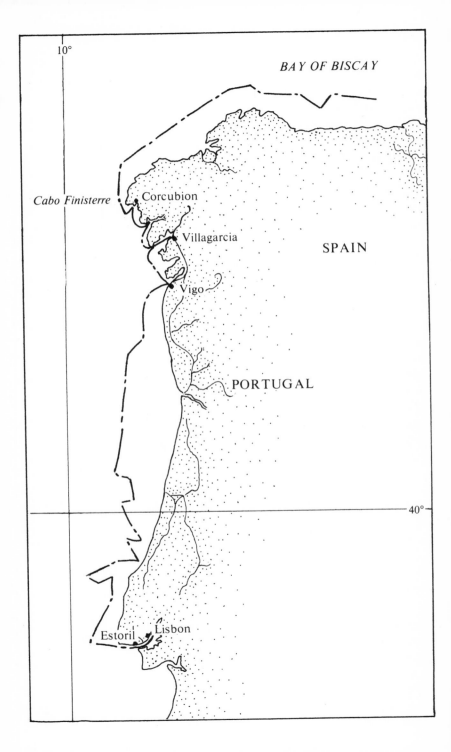

scenery. The barometer fell slowly and persistently and shortly before dawn the wind rose from a new quarter.

Our luck with weather at sea was not as good as our luck when coasting or ashore. Again we faced headwinds. On the second day a sharp southerly gale set in and simply would not let up. We decided to head toward Lisbon, a harbor of refuge. No other suitable harbors are found along the Portuguese coast. The few small fishing villages with harbors require local knowledge and are unsafe to attempt in heavy weather.

In the howling southeast gale that we now faced, our vessel labored as seas built up quickly. By noon the second day, we had covered 120 miles on course, averaging 5 knots. Gradually the wind hauled to due south and increased, heading us. The going was hard as we were forced to tack repeatedly. In the evening we considered turning back to Bayona, then 175 miles downwind, or continuing to the harbor of Lisbon and the Tagus River, 100 miles to windward. We had a stout ship, we were all rested, and we wanted to get south; by unanimous choice we continued beating to Lisbon. Those 100 miles took two and a half days as we tacked 160 hard miles to windward.

One night we lay quietly hove-to, inshore of the shipping lane, on an offshore tack for a needed rest while the wind whistled in the rigging at 35 knots. With the staysail backed to windward, the mizzen free, and the helm down, *Mischief* lay comfortably beam to the sea, footing at 1 knot. Another evening we hove to at sea for two hours to prepare and eat dinner comfortably.

Late afternoon on September 24, we rounded Cabo Raso and reached the broad mouth of the Tagus River, which leads to Lisbon about nine miles upstream. On our port hand lay Cascais and Estoril, posh playgrounds of European royalty and other notables. Their obvious comfort and security seemed unreal, even immoral, to us in our fatigue. We had earlier surmised that such places must have protected yacht basins and anchorages, although the Coast Pilot made no mention of this. Gayle and I had a private conference below at the chart table reviewing the U.S. Pilot and Sailing Directions covering this area. They contained worrisome details about the strong tidal currents and other navigational dangers at the river estuary. One such alarming comment from Sailing Directions was that it is not uncommon for ships entering the Tagus River against the tide to lose steerageway.

The only reasonably safe anchorage seemed to be Estoril at the mouth of the river on the north bank, but it was a bad lee shore. We began to wish that we had never planned to come there. We decided to go in and have a cautious look at Estoril, provided we could get back out with daylight left. Otherwise we planned to choose a spot off nearby Cabo Raso to heave-to for the night, then enter the next day with a favorable tide to look for a yacht basin somewhere upriver. High tide that evening was at 1632 hours. The endless beating into strong seas and winds had left us too tired to push on to Gibraltar, which would require 100 more miles of the same before rounding Cabo St. Vincent. And we had no time to wait for a change in the weather.

The sun was setting as we approached the north branch of the river estuary, wary of rocks and shoals that divided the north and south branches. (Flying out of Lisbon a few days later, we were startled to see a large motor yacht stranded on these rocks, the sea pounding it to pieces.) The U.S. Pilot states that all vessels entering Lisbon are required to take on a local pilot at the river mouth. Of course this does not include yachts, but soon we spotted a black 40′ vessel that looked like a seagoing tug. With glasses we observed the word *"Pilotos"* in large letters on the hull. That settled it. I would get them to direct us to a safe anchorage.

With *Mischief* dead in the water near the pilot boat, we rolled deeply while trying to carry on a conversation. The men on the pilot boat spoke in Portuguese, which we could not understand. Then, to our relief, one of the men spoke to us in English. He directed us to the anchorage off Estoril; thanking them, we started off in that direction, rather unsurely. Shortly, a launch put out from the pilot boat. A pilot, dressed impeccably in a dark business suit and necktie, stood in the bow of the small boat and spoke to us in English, advising us not to go on into Estoril alone. Under these conditions, we discussed taking him aboard as pilot. My crew, Gayle in particular, was anxious to hire him. Being a cautious spender, I asked his fee, thinking there might be a minimum based on 100 tons of ship or the like, and for that amount we could jolly well go out and heave-to. Gayle whispered with uncommon impatience, "Dick! What a time to talk price!" The pilot's answer was to ask our tonnage, our draft, and our speed. He said the charges were out of his hands and established at headquarters, but he assured us they would be reasonable. I hired him. (The pilot service later declined to be paid for this assistance.)

By now it was getting dark, shore lights were winking on in the comfort of nearby Cascais. The pilot came aboard with a black suitcase containing papers and a uniform, but he never changed from his business suit. When the men from the pilot boat had asked our speed earlier, I had optimistically answered "seven knots." I now ate those words. The pilot told us that the tidal current, now beginning, would build to a peak of five knots and that our destination was nine miles upriver. *Mischief*'s small diesel, flat out, pushed us only six knots through the water. Still, in three hours, making roughly five, three, then one knot over the bottom, we made it to Darsena de Belem, located on the left bank just before reaching the large bridge crossing the river at that point.

The pilot sat beside me in the cockpit describing points of historical interest to us along the way, but my attention was on other things. This was a spectacular trip, one of the

most memorable that Gayle and I have had on *Mischief.*
The swift-running black water of the Tagus, flowing out
against the strong southerly wind, made up huge rolling
seas. Following us, each threatened to engulf *Mischief,* if
not throw her into a catastrophic broach. We had no sail
up but, as I look back now, I think we should have carried
the staysail.

Despite the engrossing navigational conditions, we were
enthralled by the city lights, the trains crawling along the
left bank, the silent flow of automobile lights winding
along hillside boulevards, and here and there an anchored
supertanker aglow with light. Far ahead of us the majestic
Salazar suspension bridge across the Tagus framed a large
orange moon spilling a golden track upon the black water.
The reflection seemed to beckon us to safe harbor nearby.
As we approached the small basin at Belem, in the shadow
of the famous monument to Prince Henry the Navigator,
a small pilot launch met us and helped *Mischief* maneuver
in the close quarters inside.

We spent five days snugly in Lisbon while the south
wind blew hard. The small basin was overcrowded with
yachts, the local boats occupying all available berths.
Making the best of this, we rafted together with five
foreign yachts in the center of the basin. Two days after a
sturdy 60-foot English ketch left for Gibraltar, she returned and reported that she had been unable to weather
Cabo St. Vincent.

A small Portuguese naval establishment occupied the
north shore of Belem Basin. Every day a uniformed
man—sometimes a group of two or three men—would
come out in a small boat to say that the foreign yachts
would have to leave, as we were obstructing the center of
the basin. Our Swedish neighbors spoke Portuguese. Here
is where I first learned the tremendous power of passive
resistance. Following the lead of others in this instance, we
never argued with the officer; we always agreed to get out.
But with no place to go, we never did. Each day the game

was played anew. A shoulder shrug and an innocent smile have a finality against which no adversary can prevail.

It became clear that we would not be able to reach the Balearics on schedule, as I had to fly home in early October. So on October 1, a professional ferry crew arrived from England. The delivery crew would take *Mischief* to Palma de Mallorca, 750 miles away in the Balearic Islands, arriving, if all went well, by the middle of the month. About then Gayle and I would return from the States for the next voyage of *Mischief*, across the Mediterranean Sea.

8

Arranging personal affairs for world cruising

In mid-October, after flying to Mallorca, we prepared to set off on a meandering 1,134-mile cruise to Piraeus, Greece. Everything had to be shipshape. But Gayle and I believe that it takes much more than a tight ship for an older couple to enjoy completely the pleasures of world cruising. There is nothing as unsettling on an extended voyage as loose ends in one's family or financial affairs that must be attended to quickly—across thousands of miles of ocean! This is, of course, a personal subject, and it would be presumptuous of me to think that everyone should do as we did. But having made that caveat, I must note that there is a certain similarity among the problems everyone faces in arranging personal and financial affairs. The solutions we found may provide other cruising people with ideas and options.

One of the reasons Gayle and I like living on a boat is the satisfaction of the simple, reasonably self-sufficient and independent existence it offers; it is a life obviously stripped of the stresses, complexities, and artificialities of urban living. Anyone who has pursued a busy professional or business life, raised a family, and then reached a point where he can live on a boat and voyage afar must take calculated and not merely casual steps to secure peace of mind in his new environment. This requires organizing one's personal, business, and financial affairs in a manner which makes them reasonably self-tending.

One thing that must be learned as a family multiplies and disperses geographically is that there are practical and philosophical limits beyond which one cannot carry family responsibilities. It often seems that the direction of responsibility in a family reverses as the years tick by. When I am cruising afar I think there is more reason for my children to be worried about *me* than I about them. But in fact none of us truly worries about the others, although we keep in touch as best we can.

Maintaining responsibility for a business at home is incompatible with carefree living and cruising. You simply cannot straddle both worlds; you must accept the fact that long-term cruising requires getting out of the rat-race completely. If not, you will never enjoy it. The only kind of business to be concerned with — as a necessary minimum — is personal business, specifically management and safety of assets at home and the flow of income necessary to support liabilities and living expenses. Obviously these matters should be arranged so that they are self-tending. With a little ingenuity and know-how, you can accomplish this.

If a person is fortunate enough to have important and diverse property and securities, these can be put under various forms of management contracts providing professional supervision. The costs are often tax-deductible, and the peace of mind is priceless. At remarkably small cost you can place investment securities in a voluntary and revocable trust at a bank; the bank then exercises full management power. A reputable stock-brokerage firm with whom you have done business will hold your securities in a custodial account, without management, at no cost. In either case, income can be credited to a designated account at a bank anywhere in the world. For some, the safest and easiest solution is to convert investments or savings into a combination of time deposits and U.S. Government securities. For obvious reasons, you should rid yourself of all investments that are speculative, time-oriented, or in need of special attention.

While cruising, I prefer to have more financial liquidity than I might require living ashore. Some major expense is always an unpleasant possibility. Set your own amount for an emergency reserve. A wire or radiotelephone call should be enough to provide funds quickly wherever you are. Such standby arrangements can be made with a corporate trustee, your bank at home, your stockbroker, or an attorney.

Before we left on our voyage, I arranged several forms of liquidity appropriate for us: savings deposits in our bank at home, subject to immediate withdrawal by Gayle or me; a time deposit with our bank in Amsterdam, against which I had a line of credit available by telephone for transfer to any designated bank; a number of $500 travelers checks carried aboard the boat for special needs, two in Gayle's name; a larger-than-normal balance in our joint checking account at the bank at home, against which either of us could draw by check at an accommodating foreign bank or at an American Express office. When we needed extra money, I used this last method most often.

There were several other sources from which I could borrow money if needed. Most travelers are familiar with the credit plans by which a designated bank will automatically make a loan, usually up to $5,000, to pay charges accumulated on a credit card which are not paid by the cardholder within the customary 30 days. (This would not help in a remote place where the credit card could not be used.) On most cards you can get a liberal cash advance, provided you can find a branch office. One such card is a good thing to have.

By leaving securities with a stockbroker and arranging a margin account in advance, you can borrow funds from

115

the broker at a distance and remit them by wire transfer to any designated bank in the world for your credit, all in a matter of perhaps one week.

About half the long-term cruising couples we have met continue to own a home somewhere ashore. Of course the most desirable plan is to lease the property, for its protection as well as for the income. An agent will manage it, arrange repairs, and collect rents for a fee of 12 to 15 percent. We had no home ashore when we were first cruising and living aboard *Mischief,* but now we have a pleasantly small condominium apartment in Coral Gables, which we can lease when cruising. If not leased, an apartment of this type can easily be left for extended periods without worry.

Certain expenses at home require more prompt attention than normal billing and mails permit. Examples are premiums for various types of insurance, and mortgage and interest payments. I made arrangements in advance through my bank to authorize specified insurance companies and institutional lenders to draft a designated deposit account in my name at the bank on the dates specified payments became due. This system avoided the risk and consequences of default by late payment, provided, of course, there is enough money in the account. I also arranged with the bank and with agents paying corporate dividends or interest that these payments go directly to the bank for credit to my account. This avoided having dividend checks chase me around the world, a certain number inevitably being lost in the process. Of course, if all one's securities are in a custodial or trust account, all of the income may be directed under one instruction.

My pension payments were credited monthly to a joint checking account at my bank. From this account we paid bills as they caught up with us and periodically replenished our shipboard supply of travelers checks and currency. Income from other sources was credited directly to a special joint savings account, where it accumulated and drew interest until needed. (This was the account on which draft authorizations were arranged for periodic payment of insurance, mortgage, and interest obligations.) Thus as we happily cruised in remote areas, we kept our own handling of finances to a tolerable minimum.

Banknotes can be exchanged for another currency after you leave a country, but not coins. We often seemed to amass quantities of local coins in a short period of time, since it was easier to offer a banknote and receive change in payment for something when unsure of the price and local currency denominations than to count out the exact change in the first place. But we always tried to consolidate our local coins into banknotes before leaving a currency area.

For carefree cruising and living on a boat, communications is an important subject and deserves careful thought and advance planning. Mail is the obvious medium. We learned that a post office box at home is an ideal arrangement. The post office held our accumulated mail until dates that we specified in writing in advance and periodically updated. On each such date a postal agent at home, with whom I became acquainted for this purpose, packaged all first-class mail into one bulk envelope container. This he forwarded as directed, at no expense if within the United States and at my expense when overseas. For this latter purpose I provided cash in advance.

A yacht club is a better address for mail than General Delivery or a friend's home. Yacht club personnel are familiar with the unpredictable movements of sailboats and will hold almost indefinitely mail addressed to a transient yacht. A package of mail forwarded from home might be addressed as follows:

U.S. Yacht *Mischief*—in transit
Richard J. Vogt, Owner-Captain
c/o Piraeus Yacht Club
Piraeus, Greece

Hold for arrival about May 15.

Lloyd's Register of Yachts has a list of yacht clubs, with their addresses, in the back of the book. Lloyd's Register of American Yachts similarly lists yacht clubs in the United States and Canada.

General Delivery postal practices vary around the world, but for the most part unclaimed letters and packages are held for a limited time, then destroyed. If for some reason we missed a mail port, the yacht club there could usually be persuaded by telephone to forward our envelope. An alternate choice in forwarding or receiving mail is to use a port director's office address. We tried this when there was no other choice but found the results unpredictable. There were times when a boarding officer, inspecting the yacht on arrival, brought our mail out to us from the port director's office. Yet at other times we were not even able to find a place locally designated as the "port director's office."

It is usually a mistake to give correspondents a mail-port address, and we seldom did this unless we were then prepared to wait for the arrival of a particular letter. As a rule we tried to get mail once a month and were usually able to arrange it that way.

Another dimension of communications is radiotelephone. *Mischief* has a single sideband transceiver. Equipped with crystals from 4 to 22 MHz, this is suitable for long-range communication with specified high-seas telephone-company stations in Europe and in the continental United States. When radio communication is established with one such station, a land-line patch then completes the local connection. However, this is an expensive way to telephone from a yacht, and tariffs have been increased to

118

a point where it is cheaper to telephone overseas from a land station. Of course, that is often either impossible or grossly inconvenient, considering time-zone differences and access ashore by boat. I believe the solution is to install and license a ham radio station in addition to a radio-telephone. Having both would certainly contribute to peace of mind.

In summary, Gayle's and my formula for carefree living on a boat while long-distance cruising is to be able to know that our families are well, self-sufficient and under each other's watchful eyes; to have so arranged our personal finances and property that such matters become self-tending while providing income; and to have the ability to communicate by mail and radio. Beyond that, it is up to us to make the most of the special environment that living on the boat offers.

I have observed that people rarely give up cruising because of storms, hardships or dangers. Nor are they likely to give it up because of money needs, since one can meet these needs along the way, as many young folk do. A more likely way to kill the desire to live and cruise on a sailing boat is to find the ties at home too binding to escape and the inconvenience of maintaining these ties from a distance too annoying to bear.

But there is another side to this situation. One of the great joys of long-distance cruising for Gayle and me is the chance to renew family ties and the bonds of friendship on shipboard. Many of our fondest memories of *Mischief*'s voyages are the times we shared our experiences with those we invited aboard. There are also practical considerations. During longer stretches at sea, extra hands ease watch-duty, and more than once they helped solve mechanical or navigational problems. One young man was so enthusiastic about sailing aboard *Mischief* that he was forever polishing, scrubbing, and fixing things. Another young shipmate kept *Byboot*'s outboard in fine tune.

119

Gayle and I prefer not to undertake passages of more than 600 miles with only the two of us on board. At an average speed of 5½ knots that distance represents 108 hours under way, watch-on-watch, equivalent to four nights and five days. Of course, with a proper watch routine and self-steering, there is no reason that this cannot be carried on indefinitely. Many couples do so by choice, but for us long two-handed passages become monotonous and tiring. For long passages we think three is an ideal number on board, although for the Atlantic crossing we had a total of four. We never undertake sail changes with only one person on deck. To avoid disturbing the sleep of the off-watch, we often shorten sail before sundown.

In practice two of us alone seldom make passages requiring more than two consecutive nights (and three days). This is equivalent to 60 hours under way. At an average speed of five or six knots this gives a convenient range of 300 to 360 miles, which is adequate for all except occasional necessary ocean passages.

When inviting friends or family aboard for any extended period of time, Gayle and I send a note to them confirming our rendezvous plans and our general cruise plan while they are aboard, and including both general and specific suggestions about equipment and clothing to bring along. In this way we don't have to face hard suitcases or high-heeled shoes when guests arrive—and don't have to lend someone our favorite sweaters on a chilly evening. Several months before Dick Jr., his wife Susan, my nephew Peter, and his wife Susan were scheduled to join us at the yacht basin in Vouliagmeni, Greece, I sent them such a note. Here are a few excerpts:

"Vouliagmeni . . . is 15 kilometers south of Athens. The international airport lies between Athens and Vouliagmeni, about 10 kilometers distant. Taxis are cheap in Greece and that would be the best way to come. . . . Our present plan is to terminate the cruise at Mykonos. This should be sometime around April 21 or 22, give or take a couple of days, depending on the convenience and wishes of the crew.

"At sea or during those twilight Happy Hours on deck, it is often chilly. Some warm clothes are in order in any season. . . . We try not to look scroungy as we live aboard. Thus we look better to each other and probably feel better. . . . We eat well and comfortably, occasionally with wine and the best ship's china. . . . Excursions ashore usually require sturdy and comfortable walking shoes . . . also what I call an 'instant dress-up' combination for dinners ashore. For this I wear clean khaki slacks, soft-soled deck shoes, a cotton turtleneck (as a compromise between necktie or hairy open-necked shirt), and either my 'old' or my 'good' blazer. . . . To enjoy themselves ashore, visitors are well advised to dress inconspicuously.

"*Mischief* has a well-stocked medicine locker, but bring your own prescriptions, if you need any. . . . Laundry facilities are limited to the occasional loads done overnight at a small town, or done yourself aboard *Mischief* (light on the fresh water for this). Carry enough changes to get you through washings. . . . Though I don't think you need shots, I want everyone to have an up-to-date tetanus booster.

"Be sure you carry your gear in soft luggage or duffle bags. The best buy I know of is the so-called 'parachute bag' you can get in Army-Navy stores. . . . Communication with the outside world is difficult—but possible. We do have a heap of radio equipment, including a long-range single sideband. For an airmail address, use: [your name], U.S. Yacht *Mischief* (in transit), Harbormaster, Mykonos, Greece, 'Hold for arrival about 21 April.' Our ship's radio call sign is WZL 5911. . . . "

Though Gayle and I greatly value our self-sufficiency and independence, we have no doubts that the presence of friends and family added dimensions to our cruising that we might have missed had we chosen to make a more solitary voyage. At the beautiful harbor at Paros, Greece, for example, our crew—all avid hikers—decided to trek to a marble quarry we understood was about two and a half miles away. Due probably to our limitations with the Greek tongue, we did not learn until later that the trip was actually closer to 12 miles, and we were all very hungry by noon. While we rested by the roadside, Dick Jr., armed with a Greek phrase book, climbed into a nearby commercial quarry where a lone Greek workman was having his lunch in the shade. Watching him try to make himself understood, the rest of us joked that he had been invited to lunch with the Greek worker. This in fact turned out to be the case, as the villager shared his wine and cheese with Dick.

Trudging on after he rejoined us, we talked more about things to eat and decided to stop and try to buy some cheese at a farmhouse along the path. To our surprise, we were invited in, a table was laid on the patio, and we were treated to homemade cheese and wine, bread, olives, and fine Greek companionship. *Mischief*'s crew had an instant rapport with our hosts, and after a picture-taking session, we expressed our gratitude with a rendition of "Home on the Range." This delighted the Greeks, and as we left, we felt we were leaving friends behind.

9

Anchoring and docking

For a number of days after the young Vogts' departure, it was so windy in the harbor at Mykonos that we hung on for dear life, alongside a dozen other yachts at the north quay. At one point when the wind shifted around from the north, we were forced to secure *Mischief* with no less than nine lines—including one running 250 feet to a rock on shore—and two anchors. We had already witnessed too many precarious situations where other yachts threatened us, crowded in too close, or even cast off one of our lines without telling us. We also witnessed two sickening collisions of vessels trying to maneuver in the close quarters of the harbor.

Fortunately, *Mischief* is well prepared for the exigencies of anchoring and mooring. The pleasure of lying at a peaceful anchorage can dissipate very quickly when weather comes up, and a well-thought-out anchoring system safeguards the crew, the yacht, and the skipper's peace of mind. My friends at Sparkman & Stephens said they had never designed a yacht with provision for so much ground tackle. Even so, after 30,000 miles of voyaging (at the time of this writing), I would not change it.

The following is a list of ground tackle carried by *Mischief,* with each item's use and stowage:

3 WORKING ANCHORS

45-lb. CQR plow: catted on the pulpit, starboard chock, and fitted with
    6 fathoms (36') of 7/16" galvanized chain
    70 fathoms (420') of 20-mm 5-strand nylon rope.

42-lb Yachtsman kedge: catted on the pulpit, port chock, with
    32 fathoms (192') of 1/4" h.c. alloy chain (7,500 lbs. breaking strength)
    40 fathoms (240') of 16-mm 3-strand nylon rope.

20-lb. Hi-Tensile Danforth: stands upright in chocks in the starboard mizzen rigging naked. Stowed nearby in the starboard lazarette are
    33 fathoms (198') of 1/2" 3-strand nylon rope to which is attached 1 fathom of 1/4" h.c. alloy chain
    20 fathoms (120') of 1/2" 3-strand nylon rope.

2 STORM ANCHORS

60-lb. Hi-Tensile Danforth: stands upright, firmly in chocks in the port rigging opposite the mainmast.

75-lb. Luke kedge: stowed in the lowest part of the lazarette, midships, firmly chocked in 3 pieces.

Rodes and chain to suit:
    2 fathoms (12') of 3/8" galvanized chain
    6 fathoms (36') of 3/8" galvanized chain
    47 fathoms (282') of 3/4" 3-strand nylon rope
    33 fathoms (198') of 20-mm nylon braid with core, as backup, with stainless steel thimble spliced at one end.

2 SPARE ANCHORS

40-lb. Luke kedge: carried disassembled in 3 pieces alongside and around the foredeck hatch and scuttle.

16-lb. Northill "lunch hook": carried hanging and chocked in the starboard lazarette, naked.

Simpson Lawrence "500" double-action hand-operated wind-lass on the foredeck with chain pawl and drum.

25-lb. lead counterweight "Rode Rider."

Small grapple-type anchor, suitable for dinghy and for grapple use.

15 fathoms (90') of 5/16" 3-strand nylon rope for dinghy anchor.

The weight of this equipment is 800 pounds. Approximately 570 pounds are carried in the forepeak, on the foredeck, and on the bow pulpit. Admittedly, that's a lot of weight where it oughtn't to be, but I consider it a necessary evil. An additional 80 pounds are carried elsewhere on deck, for the most part amidships. The remaining 150 pounds are stowed low in the forward end of the lazarette and under the cabin sole, comfortably away from the ends of the boat.

As the list shows, each of the two working anchors carried on the pulpit is backed by about 450' of rope and/or chain. This means we can anchor, if we have to, in 50' of water with 8-to-1 scope or in 60' with 7-to-1 scope. The light Danforth anchor has 120' or 200' lengths of ½" rode, or a combined length of 320'. The storm anchors have a 300' length which may be extended to over 500' by combining two heavy lines. All of our anchor rodes and the long lengths of chain are conspicuously marked at intervals to show the amount of line that is out. Only thus can one be sure he is setting out the scope he wishes.

Having the storm anchor rode in two parts not only makes it easier to handle and stow, but also permits versatility. For example, it provides a long line ashore which will not stretch unduly, or a long, large-diameter line to be trailed astern in a bight during storms. The ½" line in two parts is an obvious convenience for handling and stowage. Each line is fitted with thimbles spliced at both ends for quick and sure connection with a handy shackle. The only time we use the long length of ½" line on the small Danforth is when laying out a first anchor with double scope while underway; we then retrieve half the line after the second anchor has been placed. In my experience a length of 150' or more of nylon line as narrow in diameter as ½" gives too much stretch under strain; it is like a rubber band, and thus is unreliable in close quarters. The authoritative Danforth Anchoring Manual notwithstanding, I generally prefer to use heavy rope because it stretches less (although still enough to absorb shock) and provides greater protection against chafe.

A custom feature of *Mischief*'s chain and rope locker consists of two fiberglass bins in the forepeak, port and starboard, for the two working anchors. The bins are molded to fit the hull lines and butt together in a fore and aft line at the center. A mahogany bulkhead, secured by four screws, holds the bins in place. Two hawse holes feed from the anchor windlass on deck, one to the port bin, the other to starboard. There is 18" of open space above the bulkhead and over the bins for ventilation and access and a dome light for convenience. The bins have no drainage, so anything foul that comes aboard adhering to the anchor ropes or chain is confined and does not invade the bilges of the boat as often happens on other boats. The bins, of course, are removable for cleaning.

An alternative system, which I considered and discarded in planning the boat, would have been a foredeck pressure fitting for a hose to wash down the anchors and chain with sea water. I rejected this because I considered it an unwelcome complication of machinery and plumbing, and because on a short-handed yacht it is not practical for one person to crank in the anchor and wash it down with a hose. We found that with a little care the chain comes up fairly clean, and we could always wash off the foredeck with sea water from a canvas bucket after securing an anchor aboard.

The patented "Rode Rider," with its 25-lb. lead weight, is a useful anchoring accessory. With a light retrieving line attached, the assembly is fastened astride the rope or chain and permitted to slide out a controlled distance. In a congested anchorage where passing vessels could foul an anchor rope in a propeller, the Rode Rider on a short tether sinks the anchor rope to a safe depth. In a strong blow or when riding to a short scope, it increases the catenary curve of the anchor line, improving the holding power of the anchor and dampening the shocks of surge. The surface of the "saddle" of the mechanism is smooth brass to minimize the risk of chafe. Still, in an abundance of caution when I am using a nylon rode, I "freshen the nip" from time to time, sliding the device a few inches along the rode.

We carry two small floats for anchor trip lines. One is counterweighted cork wrapped in canvas, supporting a small white flag; the other is plastic, 6" long. I have painted half the plastic white and the other half international orange so I can spot it with a lamp at night. One has a 20' tail of 3/8" nylon rope and the other a similar line 30' long. We do not always use a trip line, but it is surprising how often we wish we had.

Throughout the Mediterranean, it is customary to berth a yacht stern to the quay with an anchor off the bow. Yachts are lined up parallel to each other, so that less dock space is needed for each boat. In my opinion, chain is the only thing to use in these circumstances. Unlike rope, chain lies down out of the way of passing vessels, and when it is fouled by other anchors it does not suffer from the inevitable abrasion or cutting that rope does. European vessels almost invariably use chain instead of rope for anchoring. It is said that in the Mediterranean one can spot an American yacht at anchor by her use of rope.

To accomplish the "Mediterranean mooring," you must first know how to back your boat. *Mischief* has a left-hand screw; that is to say, viewed from astern, the normal propeller rotation would be counterclockwise; in reverse, clockwise. Backing up, *Mischief*'s stern tends to angle to starboard. Therefore in backing I try to allow for a curving course to starboard and head for the portside of the target area. With this in mind, when approaching a berth we would first cruise by to measure the depth, then compute the scope, thus measuring how far out we need to drop the hook. There is always a choice to anchor straight out, to the left, or to the right, allowing for the effect of any crosswind. Generally, the best bet is to anchor straight out.

If the anchor is set well and has enough scope, the line can be tensioned, and the bow will not sag off once the stern is secured to the quay. While backing, it is the job of the person in the bow to snub and slack the anchor rode, or chain, as it pays out. Control of the bow is a great help to the helmsman in backing the boat.

One must take care not to let go one's anchor over another yacht's chain, a frequent mistake that is discovered later when a yacht tries to retrieve her anchor. I often take the precaution of streaming out a long, doubled ½" nylon line from the stern back to the quay before leaving. Thus, I can easily get back into my berth if any difficulties arise. Once clear, one end of the line is let go and hauled aboard with the other end.

There is really no defense against the risk of fouling another yacht's anchor and the occasional problems that ensue. Usually a small yacht finding herself fouled will need help. It is useful to know how to extricate a boat from such a predicament. We had such an experience at Zea Marina in Piraeus. A friend's yacht, *Takara,* lying next to *Mischief,* found herself fouled as she tried to leave. At Zea, the chance of getting fouled was enhanced by the large, circular shape of the quay. It was made worse by the fact that the offending vessel was a substantial Greek motor yacht, helpless to do much of anything to help short of coming out and retrieving her anchor—which she wasn't about to do. On a small yacht like *Takara,* the strain of lifting a heavy anchor chain to the surface will often exceed the capacity of her machinery and rigging.

We rowed over to *Takara* and offered to help. Together we rigged a four-part rope tackle between *Takara*'s mast and stemhead, hooking onto her anchor chain. We then hailed the Greek yacht and asked her to slack her cable as we lifted it. As *Takara*'s tackle two-blocked, we tied the anchor chain to the mast with a rope, opened the tackle back to the stemhead and fastened it again to the chain. We repeated the process many times, gaining about 100 feet of the chain 8 feet at a time. Finally, under great strain, the bight of the motor yacht's heavy cable was brought to the surface and secured by a doubled line from deck. After clearing our friend's anchor, the cable was let go and *Takara* was free.

The frequency of anchor-fouling in Mediterranean harbors, of course, is a natural outgrowth of the imbalance between quayside space and the number of yachts present. We were alternately entertained and appalled by the almost daily rituals of yachts forcing open space at a quay. There would seldom be a clear space at the quay of a busy harbor because everybody would be taking up as much room as he could, in order to avoid lying against nearby vessels and to have as much circulating air as possible. An incoming yacht would select a spot, let go her anchor and start backing in, whether space appeared to be available or not.

The captains of vessels already moored would immediately appear on their respective foredecks, shouting and gesticulating angrily at the incoming yacht. A hand from the stern of the new vessel would blithely throw a line to one of his abusers. Instead of dropping it in the water, as might be expected, the latter would accept it dutifully, and room would be made for the incoming vessel where there had been none moments before. Crews would get together after these wild arguments, talking and laughing together cheerfully.

For the unaccustomed, it can be unnerving to find oneself drawn into this ritual. But one learns, as I did in Pithagorian, a small harbor on the south shore of the Greek island of Samos. A French luxury motor yacht, with ample crew and guests lounging on deck, attempted to crowd *Mischief* out of the place we had selected for berthing. Since I already had my anchor down, I was unwilling to yield. To avoid collision I called to the helmsman of the other vessel to alter course and stand clear. Even as I did, we were fending off by hand. He grudgingly complied.

Even with *Mischief* secured, my anger was unabated. I walked over where the French yacht had tied up and asked for the captain, ready to excoriate him for his bad manners. It turned out that the captain spoke no English, but a Frenchman, possibly the owner, stepped off the yacht onto the quay, where we proceeded to indulge in gamesmanship. He pressed his face into mine, looking very angry and speaking French menacingly. I stood my ground. A crowd gathered at the spectacle of two men nose-to-nose in verbal battle. Naturally, it was a stand-off—to the disappointment of those who had gathered around. Even though a draw, the experience, I have to confess, was an interesting one.

Like bad weather, the occasional rudeness of other yachtsmen must be overcome by resourcefulness. It doesn't always work out as well as it did in Pithagorian. During the fall, we put into the crowded harbor at Valencia, Spain, with its commercial wharves, long warehouses, and ocean-going freighters. Finding no adequate facilities for a yacht, I finally hove-to near a large schooner berthed at the end of a small wharf, hailed her skipper, and received permission to tie up alongside. But the owner himself returned late that night, and called out loudly to us, ordering us to cast off. As I protested, he cast our lines off one by one, and an angry but useless exchange ensued.

We wandered about the harbor until we found an unoccupied wharf next to a huge warehouse; in the dim waterfront light, it looked like a spooky movie set. The stone pier was so high above *Mischief*'s deck that I could barely climb onto it from her rigging to make fast doubled lines, bow and stern, to the bollards. With nothing to hold onto, I had to slither belly-first onto the dirty pier. We set an anchor out abeam to hold her off and lay there the rest of the night. The next morning an official came by to warn us that a ship would be in to berth there at 1000 hours. It took no persuasion whatsoever to get us to leave.

Anchorages in the Mediterranean, be they small Aegean coves or harbors on the south coast of France, can be as unpredictable and unfriendly as anchorages anywhere else in the world. Small coves in the Aegean typically are deep with steep beaches. An anchor may lie on the side of an underwater hill. During thermal changes at night, the wind often shoots down steep elevations off the land. To lie safely, a yacht must tie up to a tree or rock ashore. I once met a Norwegian yachtsman who used mountain climber's pitons with rings attached for this purpose. He drove two into a convenient rock and tied in his shore lines. I plan to try this on our next voyage to avoid the kind of difficulty we encountered at Serifos, Greece, when in the early morning hours a land wind swooped down the mountain, causing our anchor to drag. *Mischief* ended up drifting onto a nearby fishing boat, suffering a nasty gash to her topsides from the spare anchor catted to the Greek boat's bow. We thus learned never to anchor close by a land mass that rises abruptly, in this case to over 2,000 feet above sea level.

Lying at anchor in a heavy blow with strong ground tackle and extreme scope for safety—for example, 10:1 or 12:1—a yacht will fishtail about her long tether, sailing off to one side and then the other. In a crowded area, this presents obvious hazards, and in any case, the anchor may eventually work loose as the boat moves back and forth. An interesting remedy is the "hammerlock." It is executed by using a light anchor on short scope to drag across the swinging arc and reduce the oscillation. I have used the 16-lb. Northhill with 2:1 scope under these circumstances. *Mischief* settled down and hung solidly on her heavy plow.

Whether well-prepared or not, all yachts must sometimes fall back on the simplest of all solutions to anchoring problems: get out to sea. I can only add that preparations to do so should be well thought out and executed as carefully as possible. In mid-September, after a pleasant week of sailing along the Côte d'Azur, we put into the harbor at Île de Port Cros, where we planned to go ashore to see the wildlife sanctuary. We made fast to a mooring maintained by the French government, pulling its heavy chain, with rope eye, through the pulpit to the foredeck cleat. We had virtually no room to swing in the small harbor, as the mooring was just inside the entrance, exposed to the north and west. By 1500 hours, we could smell a mistral coming.

The sky rapidly became overcast, the temperature fell as well as the barometer, and the radio crackled with static. Soon a sharp thunder squall swept over us with westerly winds of 25 knots. *Mischief* started to buck and jerk at the end of the mooring chain, putting great strain on the pulpit. We put a ½" rope through a link in the heavy chain and doubled it back. Then we tied a larger rope to a nearby link and eased the chain off the pulpit. There was now six to eight feet of rope between the chain and the pulpit roller. The motion eased considerably.

We lay to this all night, but uneasily. I had no way of judging the holding power of the mooring, and I felt that an anchor overboard was sure to be fouled. As the mistral developed, a blinding rain with gusty winds of 25 to 30 knots and higher buffeted us. We maintained an all-night anchor watch, and kept the engine idling in case something dragged or parted, as other yachts lay immediately in our lee. In gusts the watch would ease the strain on the mooring by engaging the engine, but this only slacked off the chain, which then tighted with a jerk from the next good wave. (Rarely in my experience has this procedure worked well.) Through the night we lay and watched while the mistral blew. By 0530 the wind had increased to 30 or 35 knots from the northwest and the seas had built and were sweeping into the cove. I decided to leave, so we discussed what our getaway procedure would be, step by step.

We lowered the centerboard, raised the mizzen, readied the staysail, retrieved the double-ended rope, and stood ready to cut the other. I expected it would take some time to saw the tough nylon even with a sharp bosun's knife. Gayle, at the helm, prepared to push the engine up to full throttle, then bear away and fill the sails; a companion was at the halyard. We would have to tack on the way out, and the staysail had to draw quickly. When all was ready I was amazed at my first experience of cutting a heavy nylon line under strain: it was like slicing a banana!

The sinking chain pulled the short rope end safely out of our way, and *Mischief* charged out of the cove like a horse in full gallop. I wish I could have seen her from the shore. We made two short tacks under power and sail. Coming about in the high wind and short steep seas, the action was a little sluggish and the sails luffed violently. On the second tack the mizzen sail came down; the stainless steel halyard shackle had bent open, and we lost the halyard. We were already clear of the land, and I wrapped the flogging mizzen onto the boom with its own sheet. We sailed and motored half a mile into the lee of a small nearby island, Île de Bagaud, but found no real protection from wind or sea. *Mischief* came about reluctantly and the staysail flogged so violently that the bale on the aluminum fitting at the end of the boom carried away and with it the clew of the sail! We quickly dropped it, put up the storm trysail, and headed for a point of shelter on the mainland about 20 miles north.

The wind increased to 35 or 40 knots, and the seas were large. Progress to windward in these conditions was very slow, so we decided to bear off and make for an alternate harbor at Lavandu. With sheets eased only slightly and a course 60° off the wind, *Mischief* plowed ahead at 6 to 6½ knots. We entered the harbor without further difficulty, found a secure berth, and within an hour had repaired all damaged gear.

10

Customs and other encounters

One dark night as we powered close along the north coast of Sicily, I was alone on watch monitoring the red light of a vessel heading out to sea. She passed a mile away to port. Suddenly, I was startled by the nearby roar of engines at high speed and was soon blinded by a high-powered searchlight from an overtaking vessel. She blacked out, slowed to parallel us about 50 yards off, and silently surveyed us for several minutes. *Mischief* was carrying a large U.S. ensign we had forgotten to strike at sunset.

I considered taking some kind of evasive action, or at least arming myself, in the moments before we were overtaken. Those thoughts passed quickly: the darkened profile of the vessel showed a gun mounted on her foredeck. Then off she roared. Though I assumed she was a police cruiser, her identity remains a mystery.

Months later, again at night, *Mischief* was anchored in a cove near a village on the small Greek island of Oinousa in the northern Aegean, close to the Turkish coast. Dinner was being readied below. At the sound of an approaching motorboat, I stuck my head out of the hatch and took a look around. As I located the direction from which the sound was coming, but could make out no running lights, I called for our spreader lights to be turned on, thinking that *Mischief* might be in the way of local fishermen.

In seconds, an open 16-foot launch appeared out of the darkness close astern. A boathook reached out. Before I knew what was happening, hands grasped the stern boomkin, and two of the six men in the launch climbed aboard. A friend sailing with us quickly came topsides and positioned himself close behind me as I angrily cornered the boarding party on the stern. The boarders made no move to identify themselves, and at one point I responded to their harsh questioning by threatening to push them overboard.

Gradually, it became evident that they were Greek customs officials and that they had mistaken us for a drug smuggler. I exhibited our Greek "transire" (a document furnished by customs to foreign vessels). To save face, they expressed their concern for our safety, and the bilingual affair soon had the air of a comic opera.

Such bizarre and unexpected episodes, though unusual, can happen to any sailor cruising extensively in foreign waters. Dealing with foreign officials on their own terms, in remote lands, and with a probable language barrier, can be a formidable undertaking for the uninitiated. Yet many cruising yachtsmen have learned that it is easier than expected, and this was our experience.

Nor are the officials themselves the only problem. There are the kindly local souls who seem to surface in every port to help with the docklines, and who make it their business to separate the unknowing yachtsman from his money by offering to handle the red tape involved in clearing customs. We ran into the wiliest of confidence men at the quay in Kushadasi, Turkey. After a hairier-than-usual docking, which drew some 20 or so curious onlookers, this chap promptly came aboard, uninvited, as soon as *Mischief*'s gangplank was in place. In English, he introduced himself by name (which, of course, meant nothing to us) as if to lend an air of legitimacy to the proceedings. He was followed by three other officials. One wore a business suit, another seaman's garb, and the third was an armed policeman in uniform. They all climbed aboard wearing hard leather shoes and showing an aggressiveness to which I responded coolly.

The man in the business suit proved to be a non-English-speaking doctor, who made it clear that he wanted to go down to the cabin for a conference. I tried to explain that he would have to take his shoes off. In order to make the point and to avoid embarrassing him, I took my own shoes off. He did not choose to follow my example, so we held our conference in the cockpit.

Through the first man we learned the doctor wanted to know where we had come from, whether anybody aboard was sick with a contagious disease, and whether anybody had died on the boat. In the background, looking pleasant but formidable, was the armed policeman. Then our genial helper explained very rapidly that as our agent, he could take care of all the complications of clearing for a $26 fee. Up to that time, we had never paid an agent's fee. I explained that I would not pay him and thanked him for his offer while ushering him off the boat.

Though fairly commonplace, such instances are not really difficult to deal with once they become recognizable, and with a little experience, a ready smile, and a patient sense of humor, dealings with bona fide officials quickly become routine. From our experience on *Mischief* in north European and Mediterranean waters, I developed four basic guidelines for trouble-free clearing:

- Have the vessel's document, certificate of registration, or charter contract, if any, readily available.

- Have passports for all persons on board readily available.

- Keep a small supply of local currency on hand for payment of the required fees.

- And, when meeting customs officials, maintain a clean and responsible appearance.

In addition, Gayle would occasionally take pictures of officials and the clearing conferences with her Polaroid; she would then present the pictures to them as gifts. The gambit proved to be a reliable icebreaker everywhere.

Mischief's documentation for her first two years, the Certificate of U.S. Ownership, was obtained from the U.S. Consulate in Rotterdam after she was launched. This imposing single-page document, with its official ribbons and wax seals, was valid for six months or until she reached her first U.S. port. In eight countries of Europe and Asia Minor, and countless island dependents, we were asked for the certificate just twice — in England and Greece. Elsewhere, clearing procedures varied enormously in both complexity and speed. What follows is an account of our experience with such procedures in the various countries we visited.

Holland. This maritime nation has an efficient clearance procedure for foreign yachts. Each vessel must obtain a *triptiek* at her first Dutch port. This transire is valid for six months in Dutch waters and may be renewed under certain circumstances. We paid the guilder equivalent of a two-dollar fee. On *Mischief*'s shakedown cruise through Dutch canals and inland lakes we were never asked to exhibit this paper; we moved about freely, including a sortie into international waters, without checking in or out.

England. Our first British port was Gosport, opposite the Portsmouth Naval Base. We arrived on a weekday morning, flying the Q-flag at the lower port spreader; we berthed and asked the dockmaster about clearance formalities. In half an hour a customs officer boarded and completed the forms for our entry. The procedure was routine, and the officer was efficient and polite. No fees were required. We were given permission for "temporary importation of a vessel for private cruising" and received a "Certificate of Free Pratique" for the yacht and those on her crew list. This was good for one month, which was all that we requested, and had to be produced on request by any customs or immigration officer, or port authority.

We cruised about freely, touched many ports, harbors, and rivers along the south coast, and enjoyed land excursions. Never in British waters were we asked for this evidence of clearance. Visiting yachts are required to notify customs in advance of intended departure; in practice, few do.

Spain. During the period of two weeks that *Mischief* cruised the Spanish Galician coast, we were unable to find a local official willing to clear the yacht. After serious tries in two harbors without success, we gave up. Flying our U.S. flag, we moved freely without incident or official entry. Sightseeing and shopping excursions ashore offered no complications. Under these circumstances, we carried our passports with us, but seldom used them.

One year later, as we cruised the length of the Spanish Mediterranean coast, local authorities showed similar disinterest in our movements, except for polite and sometimes over-zealous pressure to collect docking fees every time we came to a quay. A colorful *policia* in his tricornered, black patent-leather hat would ask about our expected stay and departure, yet there would be no request for ship's papers. Occasionally, passports were inspected on the spot, but the main interest of the *policia* appeared to be collecting the 35-peseta docking fee, the equivalent of about 60¢ U.S., for two days. (The daily rate is actually half that, but unless the yacht arrives and departs in the same daylight it is ruled to be "*dos dias, hoy y mañana.*" Often we berthed in the late afternoon for departure early the next morning, but still it was *"dos dias"* — today and tomorrow. I always argued good-naturedly, and always lost.

Portugal. Lisbon harbor imposed formidable clearance procedures for foreign yachts. A husky 50′ police launch, inadequately fendered with overhanging automobile tires and with half a dozen uniformed men aboard, appeared at breakfast-time in the little basin near the Belém Tower, where we had sought shelter from a howling southerly gale. As the vessel bumped alongside *Mischief*, one of the men asked politely but unsmilingly for *el Capitáo*. With considerable fending they picked up the owners of the five foreign yachts that were anchored with us in a mid-basin raft. We who were being taken away felt as if we should be saying farewell to wives and friends behind. Proceeding up the Tagus River, we joked and talked in German, Norwegian, Swedish, French, and English alternately, never really understanding each other. Three hours and countless bureaucratic forms later, we were returned to the yacht basin, each with an 8″ by 10″ cardboard *Declaracao Geral de Entrade de Barcos de Recreio* in hand. There was nothing difficult about this process except its unbelievable inefficiency.

France. *Mischief* cruised for a week in the French waters of Corsica, en route to the mainland of France. We did not go ashore and had no occasion to seek clearance. Arriving at the mainland in Antibes, we berthed temporarily at a fuel dock flying the Q-flag. In a few minutes it was suggested we take it down, first by someone on a nearby yacht, whom we politely ignored, and next by the dock attendant. Our arrival was two weeks after a widely publicized outbreak of cholera in Naples, a port from which we had sailed only a short time earlier. After securing in a berth assigned to *Mischief* in Port Vauban, without the Q-flag, I went ashore to find a customs office. There I reported our arrival from Corsica, filled out a brief form, and promptly received a *Passeport du Navire Etranger*.

In half a dozen harbors and anchorages along the south coast of France, we were never asked to exhibit this document.

Meanwhile, from a physician at a British hospital in Nice we received the reassuring news that we were safely past the incubation period from our cholera exposure in Naples. However, the disease was breaking out elsewhere in the Mediterranean area, so one morning we lined up with a group of Frenchmen outside a dispensary and received free inoculations. In some jurisdictions medical and health clearance of a vessel is routinely required, yet here when circumstances most called for it, no special concern was shown for the entry of a foreign yacht. Air passengers arriving from Italy were being required to show evidence of recent immunization from cholera, or were being isolated on the spot and inoculated. Such are the anomalies of clearance processes.

Italy. The small seaport town of Carloforte, Sardinia, was our first Italian port in the Mediterranean. We asked all over town without success for an official willing to clear the yacht. I took in the Q-flag on the first night, and for three days we lay anchored in the sheltered harbor while a levanter blew itself out. Sailing on to Sicily, we entered the little harbor of Porticello, crowded with fishing craft. Promptly, a police boat requested passports and my presence at headquarters. There, without boarding or inspection of the yacht, we were given clearance papers. One year later, when cruising the Italian mainland coast and off-lying islands in the Tyrrhenian Sea, we could find no officials interested in clearing a U.S. yacht. In small places local officials were friendly, happy, and hospitable. Each referred us to another local authority in what I eventually recognized as "passing the buck." At first this experience was frustrating, but soon we gave up and sailed about, going ashore freely without challenge.

Greece. The Greek police, who are polite and efficient, have an orderly system for clearing foreign yachts. In

Greek waters a foreign yacht must carry a transire which is obtained at the local police headquarters of almost any town or village constituting the first harbor of entry. Initial paperwork takes a little time, and usually someone around speaks English. The yacht must list her crew and some of her gear. For any well-found vessel the equipment list is far from complete. A cruising yacht should never have "passengers," only "crew," no matter how many guests are on board—the former entails mountainous red tape. We were issued a three-page legal-sized document with a blue cover, riveted together like a mortgage deed. No initial fee was required but small fees were later collected here and there.

At every Greek port, town, or village, whether at anchor or at a quay, a foreign yacht requires clearance. Responsibility is with the local police, not the yachtsman. An officer always comes, even if he has to be rowed out by a small boy in a fishing skiff. He reviews the passports, usually by cursory thumbing, and inspects the transire. The police always ask where the yacht last berthed and where she is bound. Although we felt free to change immediate plans, we looked upon this monitoring of our movements as a kind of safeguard.

In larger towns, papers and passports may be taken to police headquarters for review, to be returned in a few hours. In principle, I hate to yield possession of passports, and would never part with the ship's papers. So one of us would generally accompany the officer to headquarters. I once failed to hold onto our passports, and when ready to sail the next day, I went to police headquarters to retrieve them. There no one knew about them, and no one spoke any language but Greek. I resorted to gestures and an angry tone of voice to convey the need for action. With a policeman following us around, a shipmate and I searched the several rooms constituting this island headquarters, looking for our passports. We were rewarded by finding them in a bottom desk drawer under some papers. With smiles and vigorous handshakes, we took our leave from the reassured officer.

A foreign yacht should surrender the transire before leaving Greek waters. Some yachts going in and out of Greek waters cut this corner to save time, but it requires falsification of re-entry and should not be done.

Turkey. In each port, local officials gave us clearance independent of previous ones; in out-of-the-way places, *Mischief* was unchallenged. Clearance was time-consuming and required reasonable enterprise and sophistication. Occasionally someone nearby would volunteer to expedite the yacht's clearance for a substantial fee—in U.S. dollars, not in lira. The offer of such a gratuitous currency conversion usually tips one off to an opportunist. I never used an agent in Turkey, although at times I wondered if I might have been a little too stubborn for my own comfort. Modest fees required for each clearance were euphemistically called "lighthouse dues."

Turkish clearance procedures for foreign yachts are complex, no doubt because of illicit drug traffic in these waters. Officials would question us in Turkish, sometimes showing impatience or confusion at our inability to understand. Preliminary docking-clearance forms were fortunately printed in both Turkish and English.

In our first experience with this procedure, we used sign language, occasional translations from onlookers at the quay, and a little French here and there; I finally gathered that I had to go ashore and clear with the port doctor, the local police, customs, and the port director. They were all located at different places and were quite elusive. I talked to the doctor in French, and he stamped our passports. Next I found police headquarters; I was told I had not yet cleared customs and that I should return after doing so. Customs told me they could not clear me until I obtained a form from the port director. The port director noted gravely that I had not yet cleared with the police. By the time I unravelled this and made the return calls, I was plain worn out. Occasionally I was befriended by people who spoke English or French, and once by a child who helpfully attached himself as my keeper. When I returned to the yacht I had the feeling that whatever was undone could jolly well stay that way.

We had no problem with pilferage, although one hot night in Piraeus we encountered an intruder with somewhat obscure intentions. Gayle was sleeping outside in the convertible cockpit bunk and I was in my bunk below. The stranger, dressed only in brief swimming trunks, threw a scare into Gayle as she awoke to find him standing astride the steering station close by. She succeeded in driving him off with a verbal barrage. Sleeping below, I heard the commotion in the cockpit and bounded out, but was unwilling to give chase—because of the heat, I had slept below in the buff.

No harm was done. Usually the threat of unknown boarders comes when a yacht is left untended, and Gayle and I had a scheme for keeping quayside loiterers at a safe distance. We left "Tom" on board. From the dock, we would call, "Goodbye, Tom, we'll be back soon. Hope you feel better!" For Tom's entertainment, we would often leave the ship's radio playing music loudly enough to be heard on deck. It is not known how, or when, Tom first came aboard. He always stayed below because he didn't feel well. Everyone who has cruised on *Mischief* knows him with affection. Returning, we would call, "Ahoy, Tom, aboard *Mischief!*" for all nearby to hear.

Many months later, we left Tom aboard in the amused presence of another American yachtsman. He recounted his own imaginative scheme to meet the same need. He appears on deck in a long-sleeved red jersey and a fake black beard for the benefit of quayside onlookers before he leaves his boat. He always makes a point of doing something that will call attention to himself. Then he goes below. When the skipper and crew leave to go ashore, onlookers just assume that the guy with the beard and red shirt has stayed aboard.

Cruising in foreign waters can call forth a peculiar resourcefulness, and we were not without our humble contributions. As we approached Corsican waters for the first time, Gayle could not find our French courtesy flag. At the time, it seemed a bit of a crisis, as officials are sometimes touchy about such things and a local flag is not easy to buy along the average waterfront. Looking through the flag locker, Gayle's eye fell on the Dutch flag, with its horizontal red, white, and blue bands. By changing the hoist 90 degrees and cutting off a little material at the fly end of the Dutch flag, she improvised a passable, if somewhat square, French tricolor. An even better solution for the yachtsman cruising foreign waters is to buy a 35-cent full-color pamphlet published by the United Nations called "Flags of the United Nations" and to carry a small supply of cloth in each color needed.

With a little ingenuity, a lot of patience, and a generous amount of circumspection, "going foreign" need not be so problematic as one might expect.

11

Sailing the ancient seas

From Palma de Mallorca to Piraeus *Mischief* logged 1,134 miles. With the exception of a mistral we encountered off Minorca, the weather was consistently like fall in North Carolina. It was cold on night watches, and below we slept under quilts; in the warmth of midday, we shed our clothes to sunbathe. We enjoyed the best sailing yet with the new boat. On many occasions *Mischief* showed the turn of speed her designer promised, and we often registered over seven knots without pressing. We used all her good-weather sails, including the spectacular blue-yellow-and-white-striped Jeni-Wings.

Other times we powered in flat calm, steering with the autopilot hour after hour. Such times provided welcome leisure for small chores, for reading, writing, napping, and for Gayle to bake her delicious fresh bread. *Mischief*'s self-steering ability depended on wind and sea conditions and worked best when we were motorsailing. Thus we tended to hand-steer a good part of the time, which we both enjoy. It is only with the helm in hand that one feels the full glorious sensation of sailing. On night watches we steered by autopilot when only two of us were on board, even if it meant running the engine at low rpm to give the

147

trim-tab needed extra thrust. Thus the night watch could make a hot drink below and could move about to reduce fatigue or drowsiness.

Our unusual fuel capacity was especially comforting. With her diesel tank full, *Mischief* carries fuel for 270 hours of steaming at a cruising speed of about 1900 rpm. At 5½ knots, that's a range of 1,500 miles under power, substantially greater than many motorsailers; this allowed a welcome independence from hard-to-use or inaccessible fuel sources.

We did occasionally stumble upon fuel when we least expected to. At Cagliari, Sardinia, one Pia Paula del Vicario, who had helped with our docking lines, introduced himself and offered to take us to a source of diesel fuel. In moments, a startled American skipper was flying down the quay on the back seat of del Vicario's motorcycle. After a turbulent conversation in a back alley between del Vicario and a local garageman, punctuated variously by gestures of dismay, anger, and impatience, the Sard garageman finally smiled and said something to me in a soft, polite voice. Del Vicario translated: "He agrees to deliver the fuel."

While leaving Sardinia we had a brush with disaster. As we sailed across Carbonna Bay, the wind was fresh, but right on the nose. The chart showed a cove, deep in the bay, tucked in behind some small, rocky islands, a five-second white flasher marking its position onshore. We decided to go in for the night and wait for a fair wind to Sicily. Twilight was short. In the early darkness we sailed slowly across the bay under reduced sail, looking for the five-second light. Eventually, we came to the point at the end of the bay, a formidable headland with a prominent coastal lighthouse. We figured the light must have been out, but decided to proceed to the anchorage anyway.

Reversing our course, we handed sails and motored slowly, taking danger bearings on the largest of the rocky islands. After this we laid a course to follow for two measured miles, at which point we would have cleared the big rock a mile off, and could make a 90-degree turn to starboard to follow the shore around into the cove. In time, we made our turn and were closing with the land slowly. Gayle and I were both on deck, with Gayle at the helm. It was well past dinner time, and we were hungry. In order to see into the darkness better, we were moving without running lights, but as a precaution, I stood by with our powerful Cibi quartz spotlight. At one point I spotted a dark object about 30 yards off our starboard quarter that seemed to be a fishing dory. I turned the Cibi light on it and saw that it was a rock! Quickly, I played the light around the adjacent area and discovered to my horror that we were motoring about three boatlengths away from a sheer rock wall—dead ahead.

"Hard to port—90 degrees!" I shouted back to Gayle. "Make it 180! Slow!"

Gayle swung *Mischief* around gently and we retraced our path out of the dangerous rocks. With weak knees, we realized that we had been set by a current off to starboard and had used up our safety margin. On the next try we entered the cove without further incident.

The 175-mile sail across the Tyrrhenian Sea to our Sicilian landfall was well protected from the winter storms that originate in the western Mediterranean. The second afternoon at sea we sighted land, and the experience was one of the most dramatic of the cruise. Towering mountains, unseen until we were too close to believe our eyes, were shrouded in a haze which at times revealed only parts of the landscape. At one point, we counted seven distinct layers of coastal mountains spreading into the rugged interior. At sea it was sunny and clear. A feeling of mystery overcame us, and for a time we could believe the mythical lore of fearsome creatures dwelling in these mountains. By use of dead reckoning and occasional radio beacons, we made our landfall right on the nose.

Our experience cruising the north coast of Sicily soon persuaded us to press on to the Ionian islands. The Sicilian coast proved more picturesque from sea than close in. The smaller villages are, for the most part, poor and dirty. Open sewage gutters are common. The passage to Greece included the famous Messina Strait, where we were forced to tack against a 25-knot headwind. We passed Scylla rock and the Charybdis whirlpool, and reflected on Ulysses as we maneuvered to keep out of the way of the modern ferries that cross back and forth from the Italian mainland to Sicily. (Indeed, the following day, according to a later news report, there was a disastrous collision in broad daylight, sinking one ship with a loss of 14 lives.)

No observant visitor could possibly escape the contrast between Sicily and the Ionian islands of Greece, where eveything is spotlessly clean. I had cruised in Greece years before on a friend's yacht and found it largely unchanged.

Moving eastward through the corridor of the Corinth Strait, we enjoyed beautiful mountain scenery on both sides, fresh winds, and good sailing. I had been warned of a strange meteorological phenomenon in these waters, and several times we experienced it. Winds change suddenly, in both direction and force, then die, then come up again abruptly. For an alert crew, there is no problem, but it is often a surprise. Whitecaps appear on the water ahead or off either beam, and the new wind is felt—often up to 30 knots.

At the entrance of the Corinth Canal, *Mischief* stood her position in company with a Turkish freighter of dubious ancestry and a Russian ship; all vessels were circling and drifting while waiting for the red flag on the nearby control tower to change to green. *Mischief,* first in line, deferred to the Turkish vessel, eschewing the lead position through the narrow canal. An attendant emerged from the tower and vigorously waved us up to the maximum 6 knots allowable. Midway along the sheer, high walls, workmen on scaffolding saw our U.S. flag flying, and for a moment all work came to a halt. Friendly Greeks, who had perhaps spent some time in the U.S. themselves or had families there, called out in a hail of Americanese:

"Hallo!" "Brooklyn!" "Hot dogs!"

Mischief wintered for two months in Vouliagmeni, where we were joined by the younger Vogts in early April. We then sailed a U-shaped track, visiting seven of the western Aegean islands called the Cyclades: Kea, Serifos, Paros, Ios, Thira, Naxos, and Mykonos. Each of the islands is different. The Aegean is a paradise for amateur explorers and history buffs; we spent many enjoyable hours clambering over the hillsides, examining historical landmarks and archeological sites, or simply relaxing at idyllic anchorages and quayside tavernas. Distances are short among the islands. In 18 days, our log covered only 225 miles.

Cruising through the Greek islands, we further refined some of our basic procedures. To avoid losing clothes in remote places whose economies we stimulated by sending laundry ashore, we learned to provide an inventory in the local language. Gayle would make out a list in Greek, following a Greek-English laundry list she had saved from Vouliagmeni. The practice helped the launderer sort out laundry from various yachts, helped us check for missing items, and generally kept people a little more on their toes than otherwise. Most of our launderers picked up our laundry themselves, washed it at their homes, and delivered it directly to the yacht.

We never had trouble finding good drinking water. Getting it to the boat, on the other hand, was sometimes a problem. At Kos, I wanted to fill our depleted water tanks with good Greek water, but there was no tap at the quay. The nearest water was available from a streetside spigot a block away. Although *Mischief* carried 100 feet of garden hose expressly for this purpose, it was useless. We

organized a bucket brigade using three five-gallon collapsible plastic jugs, often used for ferrying water in the dinghy. *Mischief*'s water-tank capacity is 180 gallons. We must have made at least 30 trips at five gallons each. It was exhausting work, but the job was done.

The harbor at Ios (which is one of the most beautiful of the Greek islands and the birthplace of the poet Homer) was too deep to be a good anchorage, and a kindly Greek solved our problem by offering us his mooring. That evening we had a dress-up dinner in the cockpit, with a tablecloth and a swinging oil lantern as a chandelier. During dessert, the local ferry came into the harbor, dropped its anchor, and started to turn, coming directly toward *Mischief* to fetch up and swing. There were various reactions among the crew. Gayle left the cockpit hastily, evidently prepared to go overboard before the collision. One of our guests watched in hypnotic fascination, as if he were about to be struck by a cobra.

"There is no hope . . ." he muttered, only half in jest.

He managed a weak laugh as the ferry's high bow loomed closer and closer. The rest of us, grimly transfixed, hoped the ferry captain knew what he was doing. I remember expressing the view that he did, in an effort to be reassuring. He did. Just soon enough the ship fetched up on her anchor, swung around, and backed to the pier.

Kos, a Greek island lying off the western coast of Turkey, with its fertile, green hills, was in marked contrast to the dry, barren look of the Cyclades. It is one of the Dodecanese, as is the tiny island of Symi. We jumped from Kos to Symi, then set an easterly course through the Rhodes channel, sent on our way by a chorus of chiming bells from the twelfth-century monastery of St. Michael. The day was typical for the Aegean: clear, dry, and a little windy. Flying the Jeni-Wings, *Mischief* skimmed down the channel at 7½ knots with the mountains of Turkey to port and Rhodes to starboard.

Approaching the entrance to the harbor at Rhodes, we

sighted the *Barry,* a U.S. destroyer we had met several times, and sailed close by at 8 knots, showing off a little. Our reward was a snafu while furling the sail in 30 knots of wind. We ended up so far downwind that by the time the sail was squared away we had to motor quite a distance back to the harbor. Once there, in sheltered water between two dominant fortresses, we approached with awe the narrow entrance to the inner harbor. Gracefully proportioned pillars on both sides were each topped with the form of a deer in bronze, marking the place the ancient Colossus supposedly stood astride while vessels passed beneath to enter the harbor.

After the time-consuming process of clearing at Rhodes, we sailed for the Turkish coast. A heavy north wind came up, and we began laboriously tacking up the Rhodes channel. On one long tack, we tore the leech on our big foresail, and decided to put into the sheltered harbor at Symi. We were now back in a Greek port, but lacked the necessary Greek papers, as I had relinquished our transire in Rhodes. We were prepared to claim haven from the perils of the sea under international maritime law if challenged. Because of these circumstances, we decided not to go ashore. The next day the wind moderated but continued northerly. None too sure of our speed if the headwinds persisted, we left Symi at midnight to avoid the risk of arriving at Bodrum, Turkey, after dark the next day—even though the rhumb line of distance was only 42 miles.

Toward dawn we closed with the coastline. We were no longer in European waters, and sensed the differences. In the dry summer month of June the Turkish countryside had a gray look, while the Greek islands were brown. Farmhouses and villages along the shoreline were predominantly gray with red roofs, in contrast to the gleaming white and pastels common to the Greeks. Both the west and the south coasts of Turkey have become favorite cruising grounds for yachts, with countless bays set in among high mountains.

At Bodrum, ancient Halicarnassus, everything seemed exotic to us. A camel lumbered along the quay under its burden of freight. Men wearing black pantaloons mingled with others in Western dress, and many of the women kept the lower part of their faces covered in the Moslem tradition. Later, we climbed a nearby hill to get a better view of the harbor in the lengthening afternoon shadows. The setting sun threw warm highlights onto the tall, sleek, and brightly painted minarets. As we listened in fascination, the muezzins began their twilight call to prayer, a sudden flood of chanting electronically amplified from the rocket-like towers. Enthralled, we could only watch in silence.

From the coast of Anatolia and the adjacent islands of the Aegean, *Mischief* sailed westerly across open sea toward the Sporades Islands of Greece. We cruised leisurely through this area, touching various places along the south coast, or leeward side, of the archipelago. The northwest Aegean is a windy area, and its shores tend to be inhospitable, particularly the northeastern shore of Euboea and the mainland coast of Thessalonika, lying to the north. There the land exhibits a magnificent range of mountains, including Mount Pelion (5,100 feet) and Mount Olympus (9,600 feet). A cruising yacht is well advised to deny herself the best views of the mountains from offshore and enjoy the lee on the south sides of the Sporades Islands. This was particularly important at the time of *Mischief*'s passage through here in early June. The summer meltemi season begins July 1.

The nearby coast of Euboea, known as the Magnesian coast, is unsafe for boats, as in season the northeast gales blow hard onto the land. This shore between Cape Sepias, opposite Skiathos on the mainland, and Mount Pelion to the north, was the graveyard of Xerxes' fleet in the fifth century B.C. The story of this historic event, in which 400 ships were lost in a storm, was told by Herodotus:

The Persian fleet . . . made the Magnesian coast between Casthanea and Cape Sepias, and on its arrival the leading ships made fast to the land, while the remainder, as there was not much room on the short stretch of beach, came to anchor and lay offshore in lines, eight deep. In this position they remained during the night; but at dawn next day the weather, which was clear and calm, suddenly changed, and the fleet was caught in a heavy blow from the east—a "Hellespontian," as the people there call it—which raised a confused sea like a pot on the boil. Those who realized in time that the blow was coming, and all who happened to be lying in a convenient position, managed to beach their vessels and to get them clear of the water before they were damaged, and thus saved their own lives as well; but the ships which were caught well offshore were all lost; some were driven onto the place called the Ovens at the foot of Mount Pelium, others onto the beach itself; a number came to grief on Sepias, and others, again, were smashed to pieces off the towns of Meliboea and Casthanea.*

The Athenians were so overjoyed at the fortuitous results of this catastrophe that they promptly dedicated a shrine to Boreas, god of the northeast wind; the remnants of this site may be seen today on the banks of the Illissus.

From our landfall on Skyros, we sailed a northwesterly course of about 20 miles to the small island of Skantzoura to anchor overnight. A sheltered bay there in the still of twilight was one of the most peaceful anchorages I have seen. Aside from the quiet lap of water, the only sounds were of an occasional bird, or a fish turning lazily at the surface. Toward sundown, three small fishing caïques came in and rafted together against the shore for the night. Contemplating the tranquil scene, Gayle was reminded of Chinese paintings that contain tiny human elements in dominant natural settings—the Taoist philosopher, for example, in a small boat, or a tiny hut on a

*Herodotus, *The Histories,* translated by Aubrey de Sélincourt (London: Penguin Books, 1954).

mountainside. The three small blue, yellow, green, and white caïques and the sound of an occasional Greek voice across the glassy water of the bay had the same effect.

The caïque (pronounced "kah-eek-ee") is a boat of traditional Greek design, with high bows and a broad, flared beam. It is said that every Aegean traveller ought to visit a boatyard in the islands to get the resinous tang of pine shavings in his nostrils, and to see the ribs of a new caïque shining in their fresh-trimmed whiteness as the boat comes to life, piece by piece. Most Greek boatbuilding these days is done in Piraeus, where large yards have put the smaller ones that once flourished in the islands out of business. A small yard still exists, however, at the head of the eastern harbor on Skiathos. At the Skiathos yard, the master builder showed us a beautiful, hand-carved lengthwise section of a caïque then under construction. It served as a blueprint for the workman, who skillfully shaped the frames and timbers with an adze.

The bustling village of Skiathos has an almost Continental charm, with its narrow streets, small whitewashed cottages and many flower gardens. Skiathos offered all the amenities on a simple scale, including a hotel room we took for a day, taking turns in the luxury of its hot bath.

"This," said Nils Tellander, our Swiss friend, who joined us several times during our voyage, "is civilized yachting." At the time, we were sitting in the shade of a streetside taverna awning enjoying an afternoon snack of yogurt and baklava. Gayle and I could not have agreed with him more.

12

To Stromboli

From the Sporades, *Mischief* entered the steep straits lying between the Greek mainland and the 75-mile-long island of Euboea. This is a fjord-like route varying from two to five miles in width. Acceptable anchorages are scarce, and their availability determined our daily runs, crisscrossing this beautiful waterway. Access to this area from the sea is via the Trikeri Strait and the Oreos Channel. In the words of the Mediterranean Pilot, the south shore of this narrow waterway "consists principally of high precipitous rocks without shelter even for the smallest craft, nor scarcely a place where a boat can land."

Progressing down the strait, we found suitable anchorages on the western side of the waterway. *Mischief* sailed past the historic sites of the battles of Thermopylae and Marathon, near where the Persian fleet in 490 B.C. took fleeing troops aboard after their defeat. Negotiating the narrows at Kalkis was a unique experience. A vehicular bridge crosses there; sturdy abutments extend along both sides, almost forming a lock. The one-way width and the strong daily tidal currents make the water swirl violently at times between the abutments, rendering the narrows impassable. For our passage we had to wait seven hours for the light signal indicating slack water, along with a small fleet of caïques and other yachts.

We had logged 3,750 miles in ten months. After a layover in Piraeus to have the engine overhauled, we began our westerly passage through the Corinth Strait, encountering strong headwinds from the northwest along the way. Tacking with her double-head rig—#2 jib-top, staysail, and reefed main—*Mischief* shouldered powerfully through the seas with good speed in winds of 25 to 35 knots. This was the best sailing experience of all our voyaging. Often we made a game of helmsmanship, competing for the fastest hourly run. Since seasonal westerlies develop force in the afternoon, we enjoyed quiet mornings and planned daily schedules accordingly. We usually included a midday stop for lunch and a refreshing swim in the hot sun, topped off with a bit of cold Greek ouzo.

Under such circumstances, the days seemed to blend into one another. Time became a flexible concept. In navigation, chronometer time is the epitome of precision; *Mischief*'s quartz chronometer has a rate of daily error of one hundredth of a second. Yet we often had to guess what day of the week it was. The calendar blurred into a pleasant vagueness. Time became a companion—in stark contrast to the world of appointments and deadlines, where time can be a ruthless master.

After stopovers in the little harbor of Vathi at Ithaca, and the lovely mountainous cove of Sivota Bay at Lefkos, we blasted along in the strong winds whirling about the mountains under yankee, reefed main, and mizzen, threading our way through narrow waterways between islands and across open bays. We passed close by Skorpios, unable to tell whether Jackie was in residence, but observing the Onassis yacht *Christina* berthed at the island quay. The many islands south of the narrows between the north end of Lefkos and the mainland were well-forested, unusual for Greece. Cypress and evergreens covered the hillsides, shading the many fine summer homes that nestled along the waterfront. The scenery was not unlike that of the coast of Maine.

Once clear of Lefkos, we laid a course across the Bay of Demata toward Parga, 35 miles to the northeast, in a brisk 25-knot breeze. The small harbor at Parga is reached through a complicated entrance, and an inhospitable surge had built up inside. After a cautious look around, we anchored off, with a long line running to the quay. In so doing, we inadvertently set the stage for an awkward and amusing escapade, since the distance to the quay ruled out disembarking on foot.

Gayle and I, together with two Greek guests, dressed for a shore excursion, piled into the rubber dinghy, and rowed through the surf toward a steep little beach. A busy dockside restaurant was crowded with afternoon diners. The four of us, rub-a-dub fashion in the dinghy, were the center of attention as we reached the beach. Gayle leapt out as the bow touched sand, only to find the water much deeper than she'd expected. As she stood knee-deep, the next wave toppled her. It also lurched the dinghy hard onto the beach. One of our guests, sitting on the stern, fell head-over-heels backward into the water. It was a tribute to our mood that we enjoyed a good laugh—along with what seemed like the entire populace of Parga.

The small islands of Paxos and Antipaxos, lying some 15 miles from Parga, were two marine dream spots. From the east, the harbor at Paxos was visible across a barrier reef barring entry from that direction. The entrance, almost hidden on the northeast corner of the island, was so narrow that two yachts could barely pass. Inside, a half-dozen yachts lay stern to the quay at the village of Gaios, one of the few remaining places in Greece where the people so value their olive trees that they pass them down from generation to generation. Each tree has an identifying number that is registered in the local municipal records, as if it were a real estate deed.

At Gaios, we decided to carry out a long-delayed rigging project, installing a new halyard block up the mast for the roller-furling Jeni-Wings. With this addition, *Mischief* now has four foredeck halyards—one extra for sail changes and the others for the roller-furling yankee, the Wings, and the working staysail.

From our last stop in Greece, the island of Corfu, our Italian landfall lay 225 miles across the Ionian Sea at Capo Spartivento. On offshore passages, we navigated largely by dead reckoning, using radio beacons when available for departure and homing. In this case the light of Capo Spartivento had a range of 21 miles and would be hard to miss. To reach this powerful light during the last hours of darkness, we left Corfu at midday.

During the first night the wind dropped to almost nothing. We started the engine, lowered sails, and powered lazily with automatic steering. Gathering clouds and flashes of lightning in the northern sky warned of an approaching squall. Then a sharp drop in air temperature during my watch prompted me to put up the staysail and mizzen to be ready for the wind. Hearing the commotion on deck, Gayle got up from bed and came out to help. We sat together in the cockpit, and soon the wind came with a rain of hail drumming over the boat. We turned our backs to this stinging barrage, and *Mischief* flew along at 7 knots with her short rig. We loved every minute of it.

Capo Spartivento was rounded in early morning light. By midday we approached Messina Strait. We had been delayed for two hours drifting offshore in a calm while trying to clear the engine of a stubborn airlock, and by this margin the tide had turned against us. The question was whether to anchor somewhere and wait six hours, or to try to claw through the strait on a foul tide against the advice of the Sailing Directions. As there was no satisfactory anchorage, we decided to work our way through.

For a time I laid a course for Reggio that was close to the eastern shore, powering in a light headwind without sail. We found the back eddy I hoped might exist close inshore, although there was no mention of this possibility in the Sailing Directions. In two hours we averaged 7½ knots over the bottom while logging 5 knots through the water. Approaching the narrows, I suddenly felt the grasp of a strong adverse current sliding the boat backward and sickeningly sideways. I turned quickly, full into the tidal stream, to clear the nearby shore. We broke out the big yankee smartly and with the engine flat out tacked across the narrow strait. Thus rigged, we sailed without incident through the whirlpool of Charybdis, and for an hour tacked back and forth many times, sometimes gaining small distance to windward and upstream, sometimes losing ground. Finally we escaped the grasping current and arrived in Scylla, our Italian port of entry.

To the northwest of the port of Scylla lay the island of Stromboli, one of the few active volcanoes in the world. *Mischief* powered there over a glassy sea, circumnavigating the cone-shaped island close inshore in the fading afternoon light. Every few months the volcano spurts fire and ash in a spectacular way. With binoculars we observed the steaming bubbling cap with fresh lava flowing down a high crevass. Even as we watched we were startled by a muffled explosion and new burst of smoke and lava at the top. The entire west side of the island from the sea to the peak presented a monotone of reddish-black desolation. The opposite side was a contrast of green slopes and rolling hills covered with grass and scrub growth.

We had been told there was a small harbor by the village at the northeast corner of Stromboli. There we conned our way as close to the black sand beach as we dared, about two boat lengths, but it was 60 fathoms deep! Obviously the eastern side of the mountain presented the more stable topography, so I reasoned that somewhere along the coastline there might be a shelf on which we could drop our hook. In this search we must have made two round trips before deciding on a spot 60' deep just around the corner from the village. The breeze was light and offshore, and the situation appeared satisfactory without tying a line ashore for the short time we would be there.

As often happens when one yacht sees another at anchor in unfamiliar waters, she snugs in. We had scarcely settled down in our lonely and precarious spot when another sailboat appeared around the bend of the beach. Slowly she sounded her way to a spot near us and anchored. Before sundown, five yachts were gathered in a tight little cluster, two with lines ashore.

Throughout her maiden voyage in the Mediterranean, *Mischief* performed admirably. Besides being hauled in the early spring at the boatyard in Lavrion, Greece, for a fresh coat of bottom paint, she was in for repairs only twice. An overheating engine was to plague us until we finally corrected it in the Caribbean (it turned out to be salt-constricted tubing); attempting to fix it once and for all, we had our engineer friends at Leonidhopoulos & Co. undertake a major overhaul of our Westerbeke at Zea Marina in the heat of mid-July. Problems with the refrigeration system were also corrected.

When we reached the southern coast of France in the fall, we took all sails to the Hood loft in Nice for inspection and minor repairs in preparation for our Atlantic crossing. Brookes & Gatehouse agents from Cannes checked and serviced our electronic equipment. The Dunlop life raft was sent to Marseille for its 12-month servicing by a factory representative. I inspected all standing rigging and all fittings, inch by inch and piece by piece. One wire halyard was replaced. The French marine stores were well equipped with first-class merchandise and willing, competent staff. Between France and the Caribbean we found no comparable yacht-refitting facilities, and I was glad to have accomplished so much at Antibes.

13

Gale in the Golfe du Lion

The northwest corner of the Mediterranean Sea is notorious for rough and windy weather, as the nearby Pyrenees that separate Spain and France and the Rhône River valley of southern France combine to make a formidable weather factory. When the prevailing northerly wind reaches Force 5, it is called a "mistral." A shallow continental shelf rims the Golfe du Lion about 30 miles offshore, then the seabed falls off sharply to 1,200 fathoms. Blowing from the land, the mistral causes turbulence in the deeper waters beyond the shelf.

The course *Mischief* now followed was a curving track along the continental shelf. Inside this line, seas normally are lower. The distance by rhumb line from Toulon to Cabo San Sebastian on the Spanish Costa Brava is only 150 miles; by our curving route, probably 180 miles. I had been anxious to clear this area before the time of the fall equinox, September 23, as this rapid solar passage is often accompanied by a period of weather instability.

Weather and a minor engine repair delayed our departure from Toulon. We spent considerable time at the Bureau National de la Météorologie, where we found helpful people, weather maps, and forecasts. In this home port of the French navy such facilities command credibility. For two evenings at twilight the sky was heavy with clouds in all shades of red, as a mistral blew angrily. The morning of September 23, one of the meteorologists prepared a weather map for us, beautifully illustrated in color. He promised moderating winds and seas during the next 24 hours and advised us to leave soon or risk being weathered in at Toulon for a week or ten days more as a larger storm system was gathering force on the continent north of us. Our voyage required about 30 hours, the latter part clear of storm tracks, so we decided to make a hasty departure.

We cleared Toulon harbor at 0900 on September 23 with one guest aboard. We had fair weather and fine sailing all day. When the wind diminished in mid-afternoon and boat speed fell below 5 knots we used the engine. During late afternoon we were steering 260°, logging 7 knots with double head rig, the #2 jib top, staysail, and full main. By 1700 hours clouds had covered the entire sky; the sea and sky were monochrome gray in the overcast light, and the wind increased to a fresh 25 knots. A small land bird, instinctively seeking shelter, perched on one of the baggywrinkle chafing pads in the rigging. The bird would hang on, blow away, and fly back. The sky all around us from south, west, and north was a solid, low cloud layer with heavy gradient lines, but the barometer was steady.

As a precaution before dark, we rolled a deep reef in the mainsail. Sunset was eerie, a melange of gray, orange, and black tones. By 2000 hours the wind was blowing a steady 25 knots, gusting to 30. We handed the #2 jib and put up the mizzen; in this trim, with staysail, reefed main, and mizzen, *Mischief* balanced well. Gayle served an attractive dinner in the cockpit. We were making good time, sailing comfortably, and I felt my ship was tight.

By 2200 hours the wind and sea had increased further,

and *Mischief* was giving a rough ride. Lightning flashed in the north and far to the south though the glass remained steady. After dark the temperature dropped, and we bundled up in the chilly night air, all three of us in the cockpit. During dinner we planned night watches: Nils, our frequent sailing companion, from 2200 to 0100; I from 0100 to 0400; and Gayle, at her request, 0400 to 0700. *Mischief* handled well, but the motion was uncomfortable as seas rose and wind gusted to 35 knots. I decided to stay in the cockpit with Nils during his watch, intending to double all watches similarly. *Mischief*'s cockpit is specially designed to provide a sheltered place for a back-up watchkeeper to sleep fully suited and ready to lend assistance. In this position I stretched out to get a little sleep.

By midnight it was blowing a steady 35, gusting even higher, and seas were turbulent. Our position was along the continental shelf but more to the south than planned, due to the southerly leeway of our starboard tack (I had the centerboard up so the boat would give a little easier when hit by beam seas). *Mischief* was heeling excessively, burdened even with her reefed main, but moving very fast at 8½ knots. I dreaded the thought of taking the mainsail down under these conditions, and we continued in this trim. Soon prudence left no choice as the wind increased to 40. Gayle was called from the warmth of her off-watch bunk, as Nils' skillful hand at the wheel was essential for the dousing operation. It was a black night. The boat was lively but sensitive to steer. Moving about was a gymnastic exercise, and the spray across the deck was stinging.

Gayle and I worked together carefully and patiently. In all but calm conditions we do deck work with a safety harness and a tether fastened to the aforementioned flexible wires that run almost the length of the boat, port and starboard. It was a relief when we returned to the safety of the cockpit. We had furled the wildly flapping sail and secured the boom in its safety crutch. With shortened sail—staysail and mizzen—the boat felt much better.

The north-northwest wind rose to a steady 45 knots, gusting savagely to 50 and 55 knots. It screamed in the rigging, compounding the sounds of violence. I had to steer standing up with two hands on the wheel at all times. *Mischief*'s speed gave quick and positive control to the helm and probably was an advantage as long as she did not drag seas after her or suffer gear failure.

I considered alternatives as I held her onto the course we wanted to make good. Earlier I had started the engine to run at low standby speed, thinking if a maverick sea pushed the boat off course beyond a point of quick recovery, we would have an additional source of power immediately available. In retrospect I think it would have been better not to have the engine running, even at idle, for lines could easily have washed into the water, and the propeller could have been fouled before I could have shut down the engine. In any case, the engine soon overheated and had to be shut off. My diagnosis at the time was that, since the sea-water cooling intake is on the starboard side far below the waterline, on the starboard tack an occasional heavy roll evidently exposed the intake, which sucked air and caused an airlock in the cooling system.

In ten hours, from midnight to 1000 the morning of September 24, when we anchored in Palomas harbor five miles south of San Sebastian Light, we covered 78.6 miles through the water, an average of 7.9 knots. In the six hours from midnight to 0600 our log showed 52.6 miles covered, an average of nearly 9 knots.

During the height of the gale the seas often rose above the lower spreaders. They came relentlessly, the worst I had ever experienced. In the dark it was difficult to see well enough to steer purposefully through the waves, yet it was important for safety and comfort to do so. The process is a form of dance, the boat and the sea being partners. My turn

170

at the helm was to stretch into seven hours, although it was actually not as tiring as I would have expected. Standing at the wheel I kept my eyes to windward, with ears cocked for the hissing sound of breaking seas from abeam or the quarter. Whenever a nearby wave broke, I would angle *Mischief*'s stern toward it. She would feel the sea's grasp for a brief moment—often the wave would climb aboard—then she would regain steerage quickly. The breaking sea, now confused by the boat's passage, would dissolve in spectacular foam to leeward. We took a lot of green water in the cockpit.

Before long I discovered a wild rhythm and sequence to the seas. There would be about a full minute of confused wind-blown waves through which *Mischief* drove easily with her speed and power; then the northern skyline would begin to rise slowly, higher and higher, as a series of three large seas approached from abeam. As *Mischief* began to rise I would come up slightly with the helm, traversing the leading face of the wave and slicing across the top with no difficulty. The boat's passage over the crest of the sea often seemed to make it break. It would pass with a roar, leaving a great boiling path to leeward.

Meanwhile, as she cut through the crest, *Mischief* would roll to windward on the backside of the first sea. Then, in the trough between the first and second waves she would experience a rhythmic counter-roll to leeward. Usually this coincided with the moment of lift on the advancing face of the second wave; this new force would accentuate the roll and lay *Mischief* hard over. I thought at times the spreaders might even have reached the water if there had not been a hole in the wave trough to leeward. Even in this severe angle of heel she steered with positive control across its rising face.

The third sea, however, was usually breaking. As *Mischief* recovered from the roll to leeward and the crest of the second wave passed, the face of the onrushing third wave would dampen her counter-roll to windward. As I bore away, a roll to leeward would then be just beginning, helping to angle *Mischief*'s quarter into the breaking sea. I would call "Watch it!" and stoop over the helm, hunching my back to the sea, as a heavy weight of green water would fall upon me. Shedding water like a retriever, *Mischief* drove on almost without hesitation. The lower cockpit level would be nearly full after such a drenching but drained quickly through two self-bailing 1½" drains.

This was indeed full-out sailing, uncomfortable and sometimes scary, but I felt complete control over the vessel. Her speed contributed to my control as long as we suffered no gear failure. Perhaps we were still carrying too much sail, for strains on the boat and gear were terrific. The wind was blowing 45 knots and frequently gusting to 55 knots. Changing sail under these conditions would have been even more hazardous than before. Since *Mischief* was designed to be unusually strong, I decided to test her. We could have hove-to, lying in the path of the gale we now hoped to escape from; however, that would have required a change of sails, taking down the mizzen and putting up the storm trysail—quite an effort under these conditions—so I ruled it out.

At 0440 we sighted the looms of two large coastal lights, as we had expected. At 0455 we identified the light of Cabo San Sebastian dead ahead on a bearing of 220° magnetic, which had been our course for hours. Dawn was cold and gray, and the wind still had not let up. During the night we had joked that perhaps it was just as well that we could not see the seas, as the sight might have scared us to death. Now with the breaking dawn we could see what we were going through, and it *did* almost scare us to death! Seas were frequently above the lower spreaders, which are 25 feet off the water. Sometimes a cresting wave would strike the windward bow with sudden sledgehammer force, and spray would stream horizontally across the deck. The force of the wind was awesome.

We continued to take green water on third waves, and I tried my best to counter with various tactics. It seemed best to angle the stern toward them about 45 degrees. This eased the boat, and we suffered no harm from water taken aboard. All the rigging and other gear held together admirably, although each of us later admitted we had been expecting something to give way spectacularly during the night. We had no lines in the water and nothing on deck was out of its proper position, the latter a tribute to our careful stowage. Too often this principle is neglected on well-found yachts. Belowdeck our only problem was the gimballed stove. It had swung so far that it had dumped the teakettle down the back, which had jammed the gimbals; the oven door had then opened and spewed out its contents of pots and pans.

Soon the San Sebastian light itself was clearly in view, located on a headland 31 miles away. Our approach through the dawn and early morning hours seemed interminable. The sky began to clear, the sun came out brightly, the barometer continued steady, and the wind moderated mercifully to 30–35 knots. Shortly after dawn we had a brief and breathtaking view of the Pyrenees to the northwest, snowcapped and top-lighted by the horizontal rays of the rising sun.

Close to Cabo San Sebastian we bore away to clear offshore rocks at Las Hormigas and headed southerly for the nearby harbor of Palomas. There, about a mile offshore, seas were less turbulent and *Mischief* more docile. On the chart the harbor of Palomas appears well sheltered from northerly winds, though we were to learn that the shelter there is from the sea, not the wind. The northwest wind howled undiminished through the anchorage.

We rounded a headland and sailed toward the land. Soon the harbor opened up to the north of us. We tried to motor the last half mile to windward into the shelter of the small harbor, but the engine quickly overheated beyond tolerance, so we turned it off. The wind was

30–35 knots on our starboard bow. We were reminded of the adage that land is a boat's enemy. Ahead was a beach; to leeward, half a mile away, rocks. To windward on the right was the harbor breakwater, and on the left, inside the harbor, was another beach.

We put up the reefed main and bore away a little, gathering speed, then sailed close to the beach on the western side of the bay, came about onto a port tack, and headed east of north. With the sails sheeted hard, a strong gust knocked *Mischief* down, rail under. The crew was forward, in their halyard and anchoring stations, and all held on. Having no room to windward, I quickly eased the mainsheet and bore away. We made two tacks into the shelter of the breakwater and continued along the beach inside until we were in quiet water, then came up smartly, dropped sails and coasted toward the beach until it shelved to 20 feet. Not knowing how steep the bottom might be, we let go the working plow anchor and soon blew back on 200' of nylon rode.

Hungry as we were for the bacon-and-eggs breakfast Gayle had been promising, we decided to put out a storm anchor first. We rigged, for the first time, the 60-pound Danforth Hi-Tensile and soon settled back on two fine anchors, thankful to have arrived without mishap. While not wishing to repeat the experience, we agreed that the sights, sounds, and feelings were exhilarating. None of us had felt truly frightened; rather, we had been sobered by the circumstances and the importance of handling the boat and ourselves in the safest way.

I mused to myself that during the long, dark, wild time of the gale, Poseidon and other gods of the sea and the wind must have been pleased to see the little yacht *Mischief*, a "Flying Dutchman" from Breskens, Holland, screaming through the night, taking her crew to safe harbor.

14

Voyage to the Canaries

An air of suspense hung over the yacht harbor at Gibraltar in early November. Twenty yachts of all sizes and nationalities waited for a change in the weather to clear the Strait of Gibraltar and make for the Canary Islands. Our own uncertainty was heightened by recent international tensions from the new war in the Middle East and anti-American feelings in nearby Morocco.

Most transient yachts were berthed in the now-abandoned "destroyer pens." To us they looked crowded and exposed to surge from the bay, so we continued into an alternate anchorage, a so-called marina. This was even more crowded with craft of all kind, with no place available at a quay; but it did offer better shelter, so we tied *Mischief* to a mooring in this inner bay just south of the airstrip and under the massive familiar face of The Rock.

The weather deteriorated and the wind came strongly from the east. The next day The Rock was covered with angry, black scudding clouds. Using the dinghy, we put out the working plow anchor to windward. Soon we put out a second one, the Danforth storm anchor, as gale conditions developed. In our position we were well sheltered from the sea but not from the wind. This was a new wind for us, a "levanter." It howled across the airstrip at up to 60 knots. *Mischief* reeled and fishtailed around her tethers, but remained quite secure. We spent the time below writing, reading, doing chores, and reviewing our sailing plans.

All of the yachts were weathered in at "Gib" for five days, providing time for us to have work done on the engine. We undertook various shopping and sightseeing trips ashore, but never left *Mischief* unattended for long. Each passage in the rubber dinghy was an adventure in itself because of a strong crosswind, so we made the most of these excursions.

British names for Gibraltar's streets and public squares and the local British accents provide evidence of Britain's occupation of The Rock since 1704. Other characteristics of the populace bear witness to the eclectic nature of the British passport. Of the 26,000 inhabitants clinging to this rugged headland, a majority appear to be Spanish, and a large number, Indian. Others are the typical overseas Englishmen that one sees here and there throughout the world. Since 1967 the frontier between Spain and the peninsula has been closed by Spain as a protest against continued British rule over this strategic colony. Thus all coming and going is by ship or plane. Once a busy port and commercial center, Gibraltar is now effectively under siege—the fifteenth the Spanish have attempted in the past 270 years.

In various parts of the harbor, instant bonds developed between even the most casual acquaintances. Each skipper would ask what the other knew or planned, how long it would take the heavy seas in the Strait to subside, or when and where to catch the most favorable tide and currents. I made friends with the young French owner and skipper of the red-hulled 40' yawl, *Beydun,* bound for Madeira and the Canaries. His French tables of tidal currents had hourly diagrams which were better than anything I had seen.

Finally, with sailing plans checked and rechecked, engine repairs completed, and the boat secure, we decided to have a Saturday night ashore. Stopping at the airport meteorological office to review the latest weather information, we were startled to get advice to "leave tonight." A lull in the gale was promised for the next 24 to 36 hours, and we were told that the fearsome seas which had prevailed in the Strait for the past few days would quickly subside with the wind.

We decided to "bust out" at dawn's first light. While we had once before been ill-advised by such a forecast, before crossing the Golfe du Lion, the alternative was to risk a fortnight's delay as the renewed levanter blew itself out. This could be a critical delay in view of the late season. It was then November 11, and most yachts make this passage during October. November 15 was considered a prudent deadline before Atlantic winter storms made it dangerous for small boats to get clear of the basin of water formed by the Iberian peninsula to the north and the crescent-shaped coast of Morocco to the south.

With reference books detailing tides and currents, and with the aid of local knowledge and the French diagrams from *Beydun,* we chose the correct time for the westward passage through the Strait. Much has been written, some in tragic tones, of the dangers to small craft navigating this narrow strait between the two continents, at one point but eight miles wide. Rachel Carson, in *The Sea Around Us,* explains some of the conditions:

> The deep Mediterranean water flows out over the sill that separates the basin of the Mediterranean from the open Atlantic. This sill lies about 150 fathoms beneath the surface of the sea. The water that spills over its rocky edge does so because of the unusual conditions that prevail in the Mediterranean. The hot sun beating down on its nearly enclosed

waters creates an extraordinarily high rate of evaporation, drawing off into the atmosphere more water than is added by the inflow of rivers. The water becomes ever saltier and more dense; as evaporation continues, the surface of the Mediterranean falls below that of the Atlantic. To correct the inequality, lighter water from the Atlantic pours past Gibraltar in surface streams of great strength.

Carson quotes from a ship's log of 1855:

"Found a great number of vessels waiting for a chance to get to the westward, and learned from them that at least a thousand sail are weatherbound between this [Almeria Bay] and Gibraltar. Some of them have been so for six weeks, and have even got so far [west of Almeria] as Malaga, only to be swept back by the current. Indeed, no vessel has been able to get out into the Atlantic for three months past."*

For this same passage we now felt bold, but able.

We recovered our anchors one by one before dawn, slipped the mooring and cleared the harbor just as the eastern sky silhouetted The Rock. We crossed Gibraltar Bay in light air under sail and power. Hugging the north coast, we avoided some of the heavy shipping traffic and made good speed, taking advantage of the lull in the weather. The sea was calm, and the wind was light northerly. These conditions continued for the five hours we needed to pass through the strait.

By noon Tarifa Light on Algeciras Cape bore 028° true; we measured our westerly progress by repeated bearings there and on Cape Espartel at the Moroccan headland. The only apparent hazards were ships, large and small, including two supertankers (which require four miles to stop and have little ability to maneuver). At one time we were keeping watch on ten ships in this confined sea lane, one of which forced us into a 360° turn to stay out of her

---

*Rachel Carson, *The Sea Around Us* (New York: Oxford University Press, 1951).

way as she converged onto us and passed ahead. By 1400 hours we had cleared the strait, and as the tide changed we watched the bore approach. It was a turbulent and slightly elevated rip of water about 200 yards wide, extended north and south as far as one could see. *Mischief* bounced through without incident.

That Sunday afternoon *Mischief* left her native continent and started across the North Atlantic ocean. Our eventual destination in the Canaries was the harbor of Puerto Rico at the southern tip of Gran Canaria; our landfall was the island of Lanzarote. There we would put into Puerto de Naos, a small fishing port. From Gibraltar the rhumb line distance was 660 miles, but we would log a greater distance because we were to sail the course in a great arc. We set a course of 264° magnetic to our own "checkpoint alpha," which was well out at 35° North, 11° West. From there, 250 miles offshore, we would turn southwest, then south to Lanzarote. We had streamed our Walker Log as a back-up to the electronic log, distance and speed being such vital dead-reckoning tools.

The purpose of our looping course at sea was twofold: to pass north and west of a large, stationary low-pressure area lying off the coast of Africa, and to leave that inhospitable shore well to the east of our track. The African coast offers no suitable harbors of refuge, and severe breaking seas are often encountered over its shallow inshore continental shelf. When the African coast lies to windward, as it did with the present easterly wind, it poses no threat to a sailing vessel, but strong westerly winds are frequent in these latitudes at this time of year, and a resulting lee shore would have been quite another thing. Also, international tensions and the hostile attitude of the government of Morocco toward the United States called for another kind of prudence. In fact, we had decided that if challenged for colors for any reason on the high seas we would fly the Netherlands flag; it would be worth the argument that we were a Dutch boat. We abandoned this idea when we heard on the radio that Holland was a special target of Arab hostility. We joked about various alternatives and sailed the entire distance without colors but kept an eye out for Moroccan vessels.

The voyage to Lanzarote took six days and six nights. Our daily runs ranged from 110 to 145 miles, depending on wind and sea conditions. We were not making particularly good time. The second day out the delayed easterly gale, about Force 6, caught up with us. We shortened sail to storm jib and reefed mizzen as heavy thunder squalls began to surround us. At 0700 we altered course toward the south to keep clear of the squall line. In turbulent quartering seas we concentrated on helmsmanship, and with the addition of the storm trysail, we made fair speed. *Mischief* rode the seas well, although steering was tiring at times. Three-man watchkeeping was set at four-hour tricks during the night, with a fully suited standby sleeping under the cockpit shelter. Later when the weather improved we stood watches singly; during the day we took two-hour turns at the wheel, informally.

During my watch the second night we overtook another yacht, sailing without lights. As we neared, she showed her lights. *Mischief* altered course to hail the vessel, and she turned to intercept us. When the two boats were running parallel, and about three lengths apart, I called: "Hello! Who are you and where bound?" In response, a man on the foredeck in accented English shouted: "We are *Beydun* bound for Madeira." For a moment we were thunderstruck, mistaking the yacht's name for "bedouins." (In fact, such is the power of suggestion that Gayle said in alarm: "Dick, I can see fringe on their mizzen!" It will be a long time before she lives down that remark.) Then I recognized the boat as belonging to the pleasant Frenchman at Gibraltar, and for the next 24 hours *Beydun* and *Mischief* sailed in sight of each other until we turned south at our mid-sea checkpoint.

The weather improved and the sun warmed as we progressed southerly. The wind lightened, so we used the engine to help us along. *Mischief*'s electrical system required running the main engine about 75 minutes a day to keep the batteries charged and the refrigerator cold. The fourth day of auxiliary engine use it began to overheat, and we shut it down. I spent many frustrating hours after that with my head in the motor as the boat rolled through the seas. Meanwhile we were in kindly southern latitudes, and had enough electricity for normal use.

Sometimes we sailed quietly; at other times we lay slatting in midnight calms, searching for a breath of air to move the boat as the seas tossed us uncomfortably. In such a condition one night we found ourselves in the path of an oncoming ship, and used the powerful quartz lamp to draw attention to our position. The ship continued on a collision course, so we flashed the one-mile beam briefly onto her bridgedeck. Her response was to stop and lay dead in the water 500 yards behind us, trying to communicate by lamp. None of *Mischief*'s crew had the ability at that time to signal international code by lamp. Although *Mischief* carried an Aldis signal lamp for this purpose, other safety details always seemed to take priority. Now we regretted our inability to respond in appreciation. Soon the vessel, a large passenger ship, resumed her course and speed.

Late afternoon the following day we made our landfall. On this voyage I had planned to use celestial navigation, as our track was outside the range of coastal radio beacons. Actually, we took no sights, usually because of overcast weather, but often because of inertia. However, we kept a meticulous dead-reckoning track, and after six days of these plots our initial RDF bearing on the aerobeacon at Lanzarote airport was on the starboard bow as it should have been. We decided not to chance an entry after dark into the little port of Naos without an engine. In a beautiful moonlit night we stood offshore, sailing as slowly as we could under mainsail only in the light wind and awaiting dawn to see our way safely in.

On our second morning there, we taxied to the airport to obtain last-minute weather information and soon sailed out under a bright sun and the predicted northeast breeze. Our course now would be westerly through the islands, and we did not want to face a west wind. The meteorologists' report of prevailing northeast winds proved in error once we rounded the southern tip of Lanzarote and, of all things, the wind was westerly. We hardened sheets and tacked to weather through the narrow channel, using both sail and power. Despite successful test runs in Lanzarote, the engine overheated almost immediately, and without its aid we had to fall off and so made very little progress in light air. There were small uninhabited islands nearby with rocky shores and unknown currents and tides. We were uneasy and perhaps in the greatest danger yet encountered on this trip.

By mid-afternoon the westerly wind had increased in strength, the seas had built up, and *Mischief* had made very little progress to windward. We were about halfway from Lanzarote to our destination on Tenerife and 30 miles due north of the commercial port of Las Palmas on Gran Canaria Island. We turned south for refuge in Las Palmas and on a screaming reach covered 25 miles in just over three hours.

At sundown the wind died completely, leaving us without steerage in lumpy seas a few miles north of the port in the path of ships coming and going. We spent an agonizing nine hours in this condition, gradually working the boat toward the harbor entrance. Finally, with a change of tide at 0330, we entered on the flood with the engine jury-rigged—we poured cool water into the fresh water cooling system as fast as the water boiled away.

This experience was mentally and physically tiring, and we slept long and well into the next day. Las Palmas harbor was dirty, as any busy port will be, but since it was a major oil bunkering station, Las Palmas was especially so. There was a coating of heavy black oil over literally everything. *Mischief* soon looked as if she had been through a war, smeared and blackened. Nevertheless, we took the rubber dinghy ashore, climbed the slippery steps of the quay, and explored this quasi-African city.

15

A special mission for Mischief

On our voyage from the Canary Islands to the West Indies, *Mischief* was to be not merely a sailing yacht but a "cooperating weather-reporting vessel" under the auspices of the National Oceanic and Atmospheric Administration (NOAA). This mission would be a formidable reporting project for us; for NOAA it would be a source of timely and useful research data.

The idea first arose several years before, when Gayle and I had shared our travel plans with a local sailing friend, Dr. Robert Simpson. At that time, Bob was director of the National Weather Service Hurricane Center in Miami. He explained that a major international research project was being mounted to examine the tropical atmosphere and oceans during the summer of 1974. This project would focus on the tropical Atlantic and adjacent land areas for a study of the behavior of cloud clusters and their role in the larger circulation of the atmosphere.

The ocean area under investigation extended from the coast of Central America to the east coast of Africa, between 10° South and 20° North. *Mischief* would transit the northern third of this 30° band of latitude on her transatlantic crossing. The project's goals required a far-flung network of observers to map an overall pattern and a dense network to examine various meteorological and oceanographic factors affecting the immediate environment. A composite organization was being designed; this included land stations, ships, aircraft, and balloon and buoy systems. *Mischief* was to play a tiny role, providing weather observations as we sailed across the tropical belt.

In further describing the research project to us, Dr. Simpson explained that the tropics receive a disproportionately large share of the solar heat input which fuels the circulation of the entire atmosphere. Vast quantities of hot, moist air over the oceans are carried upward by tropical convection systems ranging in size from single cumulus clouds to hurricanes. In these systems, heat and moisture are transported to higher latitudes and ultimately affect the entire earth. A primary objective of the study was to gain increased knowledge of the meteorology of the equatorial belt and thus to understand more fully atmospheric circulation as a whole.

Our expected course from the Canary Islands to the West Indies would cross a section of the lower latitudes of the northeast trade wind belt seldom traversed by ships, even less by ships reporting weather conditions. The fact that there is little shipping in this part of the ocean is one reason it is relatively safe for yacht passages. Indeed, the many yachts that make this westward ocean passage each year are about the only vessels ever in these waters. This is the oceanic area from which hurricanes are spawned later in the year, principally during the summer months, and this would be a focus of special study by the project meteorologists.

Prior to our transatlantic brush with sophisticated meteorology, we had relied on the techniques of weather observation that sailors have always used, with the modern assistance of basic instruments and local weather reports. With equal parts of conscientious effort and constant frustration, we gradually developed practices for maintaining friendly relations with the weather.

Our major consideration was simply to avoid being in the wrong place at the wrong time. This we attempted by planning our cruises around favorable seasonal weather patterns. From Hydrographic Office publications, principally British and American, and by word of mouth from knowledgeable yachtsmen and local fishermen, we found out what times of year were best for settled weather patterns and fair winds.

In the Mediterranean, there are various seasonally prevalent winds that yachtsmen should know about. The mistral, such as we encountered it, is a north wind originating in the Pyrenees and the Rhône River valley that sweeps down across the Golfe du Lion in the Mediterranean. Though the northwest corner of the Mediterranean is apt to be unstable and windy in any season, we found navigation particularly dangerous around the time of the fall equinox.

The warm, dust-laden sirocco is a southerly wind that blows onto the Mediterranean from the coast of Africa. The strong easterly wind is called the levanter, since it blows out of the east, from the Levant.

In the Aegean, the meltemi is a strong northerly originating in the mountainous Balkans. The meltemi blows with greatest strength and frequency during the midsummer and winter months. A yacht is well advised to lay over during these months, or to move on to more favorable cruising grounds.

Without question a sailor cruising in foreign waters is heavily dependent upon his own experience in evaluating random and local weather patterns. Worldwide Marine Weather Broadcasts, a joint publication of the U.S. Department of Commerce and the Department of the Navy, lists only nine stations in the Mediterranean area that make regular radiotelephone marine weather broadcasts, and of these only three can be received on the standard 2182 kHz or 2670 kHz crystals. Seventeen other stations in the Mediterranean regularly broadcast marine weather by radiotelegraph or facsimile. The fact that most of the broadcasts are made in a foreign language drastically limits their usefulness. Of course, local marine weather forecasts are worse than useless if they are misleading or misinterpreted, but we never gave up trying to benefit from them.

While wintering in Vouliagmeni, Greece, I picked up an interesting technique from a German sailor for "decoding," or interpreting, these foreign broadcasts. He drew up a work-form with a list of Greek weather terms in the left margin, and listed the corresponding English words in the right margin. In decoding a Greek broadcast, we would place checkmarks in the squares opposite the Greek words as we heard them, keeping vertical columns for various sea areas. When the broadcast was finished we would read off the transcribed information in English. A book containing a compendium of nautical words in a half-dozen languages, including vocabulary for weather, proved helpful in this enterprise. From the book, obtained at a marine instrument store in Rotterdam, one could see that *nuage, nefelodis, die bolfe,* and *nube* all mean "cloud."

Collecting and interpreting marine weather information in such a manner obviously presented problems, but for gale warnings and other adverse weather advisories it was adequate and reliable. In other respects, the available information on "sea areas" was neither local enough nor specific enough to be useful. Too often a broadcast would be at total variance with reality; it was not uncommon for us, after decoding a radio broadcast of "wind, easterly at Force 3," to sail out of an anchorage under full sail, and immediately find ourselves burdened with a north wind, Force 5. Of course, the explanation would be that we were contending with highly localized weather almost wholly unrelated to the general area's weather pattern. My advice to yachtsmen is not to be discouraged or worried by the scarcity of useful information about local weather. With reasonable vigilance, one hears by word of mouth about adverse random weather, gale warnings, and similar advisories.

Mischief carried basic instrumentation to assist in our seat-of-the-pants local weather forecasting, as well as several reference books on meteorology. Our weather-related instrumentation consisted of an aneroid barometer mounted at the navigation station below, and a recording barometer, or barograph, in the main cabin. The barometer, of course, heralded changing local weather systems; we recorded all changes of significance in the ship's log. The barograph gave a quick visual picture of the successive changes occurring over any period of time. We also had a sling psychrometer for measuring changes in the dew point, which was of inestimable value in predicting fog, among other things. We carried an outside thermometer for keeping track of changes in air temperature, and electronic wind speed and direction indicators. With these basic tools, and our own good judgment, we compiled a respectable batting average for predicting our own weather.

There are good sources of marine weather information frequently available to a cruising yacht beyond the usual reference books: airport meteorologists, government or navy meteorological offices, and ships. Obviously, none is always 100-percent correct, but the reporting averages are good. We walked or taxied to a number of airports, as many small islands or seaports have an airport nearby. Whatever the language barrier, a look at office charts and teletype information is helpful. At a number of places like Corfu, Toulon, Cartagena, and Gibraltar, I visited local governmental or military weather offices. Without exception, they went all out to be helpful. In port, whenever the opportunity arose, I would board a ship to gather the latest weather information—often for the sheer fun of it. Off the coast of Sicily, we once requested and received a weather report from a U.S. Navy supply vessel; at another time, a U.S. Navy destroyer at anchor in the roadstead at Mandraki, Rhodes, sent *Mischief* a gale warning by small boat.

When Gayle and I returned to Florida from the Canary Islands for the Christmas holidays, our tentative understanding of *Mischief*'s special mission was translated into a plan of action for our transatlantic passage. At the Hurricane Center offices in Miami we were briefed by the director and his deputy, Dr. Neil Frank. In order not to place an undue burden on a small crew during the passage, I arranged to report only at 72-hour intervals. Each report would be in three parts: (1) the current conditions observed at 1200 hours Greenwich Mean Time (now Universal Time); (2) the same data 12 hours earlier; and (3) the same data 24 hours earlier.

All this information would be coded to facilitate transmission—a formidable task for us in itself—and reported by radiotelephone between specified afternoon hours every third day. Gayle would be the "Meteorological Officer." She would make the weather observations and code them for radio transmission. *Mischief*'s long-range, single-sideband radio transmitter would be used to reach the American Telephone & Telegraph high-seas communication station, WOM, near Miami. Once tuned in there, a telephone patch would give access to any land line we wished, in this case the office of the director of the National Hurricane Center in Miami.

I arranged that after completing each of our reports we, in turn, would receive a brief weather analysis for the area at our reported position, and a 72-hour forecast of surface weather conditions over the sea area extending 400 miles ahead of our expected course. Without question we would have the best possible weather advisories for the entire crossing. As it turned out, the weather was so stable and uniformly fair that we joked about the forecasts, which we tape recorded, suggesting that they merely repeated what we ourselves had just reported.

Through the National Weather Service, arrangements were made with the United States Coast Guard for *Mischief* to be included in the worldwide AMVER plot as a cooperating weather-reporting vessel. This program, which is of comparatively recent origin, is called the Automated Marine Vessel Emergency Rescue service, and nearly all maritime nations of the world now participate. The representative agency of each cooperating nation maintains a continuous computerized plot of all commercial vessels at sea around the world. Thus any ship in need of assistance can benefit from prompt diversion of the vessel located nearest its position. Of course the system depends upon a diverted vessel having the capability to render the type of assistance required; we agreed that *Mischief,* as a tracked AMVER vessel, would be game to give aid to a distressed supertanker if requested!

16

Transatlantic passage

The idea of sailing across an ocean always held a romantic appeal for us. It was to be an adventure, and its spirit charged the atmosphere of the small harbor of Puerto Rico, Gran Canaria, where four out of every five yachts were bound for the West Indies, 3,000 miles away.

Life in Puerto Rico, a mushrooming resort development located near the south point of the island, was pleasant. The days were clear, dry, and warm, and the evenings were cool. There was a fraternity among the yachts; westbound boats had been leaving almost every day, and when one did, the anchorage would awaken in a spontaneous and noisy bon-voyage salute, with horns, bells, sirens, a bugle and shouts of well-wishers. We felt good about the coming voyage and were anxious to be gone, but had promised ourselves to leave only when we were quite ready.

For the next two weeks, we devoted all our energy to checking off a long "ready list" for the crossing. The major areas of preparation for any such voyage were, of course, choosing the time of year with the best weather probabilities, selecting the ocean route to sail, insuring the readiness and ability of the vessel and crew, and stocking provisions and stores. Upon each of these our safety or comfort would depend. We had selected late January to early February because we knew from studying monthly ocean pilot charts and from friends at the National Hurricane Center in Miami that at this time of year the northeast trades settle into a steady flow.

The trade-wind band weaves north and south significantly during the year, and unfortunate is the westbound sailing vessel that strays outside this band. Areas of windless doldrums lie to the south, while to the north the horse latitudes fringe the great band of westerlies with headwinds which stopped sailing vessels of old. Moreover, during the time of year we chose to make our passage, gales seldom are encountered, generally occurring less than one day per month along the great-circle route from the Cape Verde Islands to the West Indies. Though many yachts make the westbound crossing during November and early December, this is not really indicative of the best weather conditions. Many of the early boats to cross are charter yachts anxious to arrive by Christmas to benefit from the holiday charter season.

Of course determining the best ocean route is a basic part of any sailing plan. Many yachts from the Canaries steer to 25° North by 25° West, then a great circle to the West Indies, which I understand can be done by steering constantly due west by compass. The idea is that the diminishing westerly magnetic variation automatically adjusts the true course. These are oversimplified directions; I have no doubt that they would get you there, but a better plan is desirable.

Our research indicated that the best route from the Canary Islands at this time of year would be a course 230° true for approximately 1,000 miles into latitude 16° North at about 30° West. This position was our "checkpoint alpha," 250 miles west of Cape Verde. From there a great circle course could be sailed through the 16th to 12th parallels North. This southerly track is important for

194

steady and fair winds. One yacht laid a great circle course from Gran Canaria about the same time *Mischief* was at sea to her south. She experienced winds variable both in strength and direction, making it frequently impossible to maintain course. About our size, she took 24 days logging 2,800 miles, while we had strong and steady winds northeast to east northeast all the way and logged 3,200 miles in 19 days!

We felt that our vessel was ideal for this crossing. *Mischief* had already proven herself at sea; all her equipment and gear were in working order, and we had essential spares. Of special interest were the Jeni-Wings carried for downwind sailing. In our year in the Mediterranean, we seldom had a chance to use these sails, which were huge 1,100-square-foot twins furled on one luff wire, clewed out to twin booms, and sheeted far aft. Tacked to the stemhead, the center of effort was far forward. This depressed the bow slightly, giving the boat directional stability and producing only a gentle roll. The large sail area moved the boat very fast.

We selected our crew with care: Mac White, surgeon/sailor and neighbor for many years, and Phil Rodgers, stockbroker/navigator and friend, also from Coconut Grove. Both were boat owners, experienced in cruising and racing. These men combined versatility and congeniality with the eagerness for the voyage shared by us all.

For an expected voyage of three weeks or less, we provisioned for five weeks with canned goods and fresh produce. Everything that required refrigeration was considered to be extra. If a large amount of food required refrigeration and the system failed, the result obviously could be disastrous. I had heard of boats running into refrigeration problems on a long passage and having to eat meat three times a day for a brief, desperate time. We carried about 180 gallons of water in three integral tanks individually controlled by valves. We also had an emergency five-gallon plastic jerry-can lashed on deck, primarily for abandon-ship use. It had a wide orange stripe of reflective paint and enough air in it so that it could float.

Two days before leaving we had a shopping orgy at the market in Las Palmas. With a small rental car standing by, the four of us scattered into the market, each with his special purchase list compiled by Gayle. Packing the car with the huge pile of produce, and later stowing everything securely on the boat, proved to be a serious challenge. The main cabin's decor was enhanced by two net hammocks swinging overhead, each full of colorful fresh vegetables and fruits, one topped with a garland of Spanish garlic and the other with a bunch of fresh thyme. Throughout the voyage we enjoyed fresh oranges, lemons, limes, melons, apples, carrots, cucumbers, tomatoes, zucchini, cabbage, potatoes, and onions.

Now four of us worked on the boat all day every day. Everything was checked and repaired as needed. All fittings and rigging aloft were inspected literally with a magnifying glass. On the day before our departure, I radioed the Miami Weather Bureau to give them our ETD and sailing plan. They relayed this information to the Coast Guard for inclusion on the international AMVER plot.

I will describe our transatlantic voyage in the present tense, as that is how I wrote the ship's log on which the following is based. In this way I hope to make this narrative of our adventure more vivid.

Departure day

Now comes the time we have long awaited. During the morning we square accounts with the dockmaster, perform our last round of good-byes, snap pictures of friends and their boats.

At 1050, January 26, *Mischief* inches out of her berth to the accompaniment of a West Indian steel band playing loudly on the stereo below, in tune with our soaring spirits topside. Soon one yacht after another joins in a curious and unforgettable cacophony of horns and bells and sirens and voices and a lone bugle—playing, for ironic effect, taps. Curious tourists stare in bewilderment, not understanding what the fuss is about. This event will rank among the high points of our lives.

Gradually the land shrinks behind; we are on our own. At first we feel a little lonesome as we lie in the wind shadow of the island, unable to sail. For five precious hours we motor, already worrying that at this rate our fuel supply will be consumed too soon. Not until early evening can we make sail. The going is slow. The seas are sloppy and confused, and Mac White and I are both feeling a little seasick.

The night comes quickly. Watches are doubled because some of us are not too alert, and we are now crossing a major north-south shipping lane along the coast of Africa. The watches call me on each ship sighting, as I have asked, and it is a busy night for all of us. We are eating a little, resting in snatches, and struggling to keep things squared away. The boat does not seem friendly. If this is the way it is going to be, most of us decide we would just as soon not go. But now, because of the wind and current from astern, we are past the point of no return: 50 miles out, 2,950 miles to go!

First day out

We pull ourselves together this morning and welcome the dawn, playing Sunday music on the stereo below. We are still tired and the motion of the boat remains uncomfortable and unfamiliar. Mac and I, on the 0400–0800 watch, decide to change sails and put the Jeni-Wings up before breakfast. This has a miraculous effect on the motion of the boat. *Mischief* changes to a soft, gentle roll and leaps ahead with power and improved speed. Through the night we had averaged about 4 knots; in the same wind with the Wings we sail gloriously at 7½ knots! The first day's run from Zulu noon to noon was only 119 miles through the water, not including an estimated 10 miles of favorable current. The sun is bright; the wind is fresh and steady from the northeast. This is more like it.

The lead-in fitting for the deck insulator of the main radio antenna is discovered broken, evidently stepped on during the night. This could disrupt our entire radio system. For two hours I struggle to make a new fitting from a piece of copper tubing; I alternately bend over with vise and tools, then lie down to straighten out my stomach. The new fitting is installed minutes before our 1400 radio rendezvous with *Rebel,* a yacht at the Puerto Rico marina. This proves a successful test of the replacement fitting.

During the day our spirits keep improving as our speed increases, but neither Mac nor I are free of *mal de mer.* Besides ministering to himself, the doctor gives me an injection of compazine. After an initial sinking spell, its later effects are salubrious. Phil and Gayle eat leftover meals with unseemly gusto. This evening Phil takes sextant altitudes of the moon and Sirius for a two-line position which confirms our DR tracking.

Second day out

The 24-hour run from noon Z to noon Z today improved to 159 miles, an average of 6.6 knots through the water before allowing for the favorable 0.5-knot westerly current. Only 2,830 miles to go. I post a tabular chart on the bulkhead, showing the day's run, hourly average, cumulative miles made to date, and miles left to go. The ship's doctor and I have both recovered.

We experiment using the autopilot with the Jeni-Wings, and to our delight it works well. Sea conditions are moderate, and the wind is dead astern. (Later in strong winds and turbulent seas we were to find little opportunity to use the autopilot, and we hand-steered the boat on watches around the clock.) Now with surging optimism at last, we all sit together in the cabin for a solid breakfast of scrambled eggs with all the trimmings, prepared by Gayle, including country-cured ham from faraway Tennessee. The morning is busy and our energies seem to increase with the tempo of our activities.

Gayle and Mac undertake their first weather observation, a two-hour project. Subsequent observations will become easier with practice. Phil and I take a noon meridian sun sight. Both observations proceed simultaneously, requiring much consultation and conversation. There will be no boredom on this voyage! The noon meridian sun sight requires either an accurate longitude to time the zenith passage or, if there is a question about that, a series of altitude measurements, which are plotted on a grid chart to observe, by interpolation if necessary, the highest altitude and corresponding time. We use this latter method, largely for practice, to obtain a good noon latitude line and a rough longitude position by time difference.

The weather is beautiful, sunny and clear, and the temperature is 70° F. *Mischief* is flying along at 7½ knots. A rollicking school of porpoise swims around the boat, half a dozen at a time close under the bow as it cuts through the water. Others leap from abeam in apparent glee at the sight of us, dive and streak past. This is a good omen, as the porpoise is a sailor's friend. In late afternoon we spot a brown-backed turtle sleeping on the surface. We pass quietly by without disturbing him. Curiously, this is to be the last sea life, except for flying fish, that we would see the entire trip.

Third day out

We have been carrying the Jeni-Wings around the clock since the first day—1,100 square feet of billowing nylon, lifting and surging. Last night we had fantastic sailing in bright moonlight, averaging 8 to 9 knots, surfing higher. The speedometer does not register above 10 knots, and often we hit that. With the Jeni-Wings we experiment with carrying the staysail sheeted hard. This seems to improve directional stability against the often steep quartering seas. With the main pulling power far forward, *Mischief*'s bow is pressed down a little and she makes a heavy bow wave. This has already stripped off the gold tape that decorates the cove stripe on the bow.

Others have complained that crossing the ocean is an exercise in boredom, but we disagree. We are busy all the time, in fact unable to do the leisure things planned for the voyage. Weather observations, navigation, watch-standing, preparation of meals, and ship's chores keep us busy. A morning sun sight confirms the DR position. At sundown last night we ambitiously tried a round of star sights, for practice, but were tired and put aside the task of reducing the figures. The day's run of 168 miles through the water is a new high, an average of 7.0 knots around the clock.

Today we make our first three weather reports by radiotelephone to the National Hurricane Center in Miami. Upon completion of the call we are elated and decide to have a celebration dinner. Throughout the voyage we celebrate at the slightest provocation. Before long, with "Tom" steering via autopilot, we all sit down together to a gourmet mid-ocean dinner complete with wine and candlelight.

Steering at night is especially tiring, and the four-hour watches are long and lonely. My proposal to dog the watches at night by shifting to three hours each is welcomed.

Fourth day out

This is not to be a good day. The first sign of adversity occurs at 0515 with the watch calling me after sighting a ship on a converging course; this is the first vessel seen in two days, a slow freighter. Only after an hour and ten minutes does she pass safely across our track ahead.

At 0720 comes the call, "All hands on deck!" These are chilling words to the sleeping off-watch. All fumble in haste to dress and report topside. The port Jeni-Wing boom has bowed severely, perhaps near the point of buckling, and we must relieve the strain. This means getting the sail furled fast. We do this in short order, then set fore and aft sails, altering course a little to bring the wind farther forward on the quarter. In this trim *Mischief* is far less comfortable.

We switch on the autopilot and discuss damage control plans and alternatives over breakfast. We decide the pole will last longer if it is straightened, and we spend the entire morning in this effort with no success. The aluminum pole is surprisingly springy. After all this work we rest, have lunch, and change back to the Wings, despite the bent pole. We decide not to carry foreguys as they make the structure slightly rigid. The compression load on a free-floating pole would seem minimal, and this proves to be the case. Nevertheless, we are uneasy and keep a careful eye on the bowed pole. All feel a great fondness for these Jeni-Wings, as they make the boat so comfortable in her motion and drive her so fast. They must carry us to Grenada, now 2,493 miles away.

Fifth day out

Last night, beginning about 2000 hours, the wind increased to between 25 and 30 knots true. With this, the seas rose considerably. Our midnight weather observers estimated average wave heights of 10 feet. Steering safely ahead of such following seas is tiring and requires skill and concentration. We continue to make excellent speed sailing between 8 and 9 knots, surfing higher. Each night-watch is glad to yield the wheel after three hours of exercise and eye strain. Still, the nights are truly beautiful.

The moon is three-quarters full and very bright, and the sky is full of stars.

The bulb in the stern light has burned out, and replacing it at sea is out of the question for fear of losing small parts overboard. We eventually choose to sail in the vast ocean at night without navigation lights, something I never thought we would do.

The day's run to noon Z today is a new record of 172.4 miles through the water, an average of 7.2 knots. Total estimated distance made good to date, allowing for current, is 822 miles, leaving 2,309 miles to go. We are 110 miles from "checkpoint alpha."

The batteries are low today, having missed their routine charge yesterday because of an overheating engine. Long ago I changed the seawater pump impeller and found the old one sound. Now we are inclined to change the pump, substituting a factory-new spare carried aboard, but we are too tired from last night's sailing and decide to run the motor until it overheats, however long that takes, giving the batteries some charge. The motor, bless its heart, runs normally for a generous one and a half hours. With batteries now full we should make a strong radio signal in reporting to NHC.

We have discontinued use of the autopilot after a couple of scares when it let the boat wander too far off course before correcting. Once it set one of the Jeni-Wings aback with great fuss and danger to the sail. We are back to hand-steering around the clock. Although it means extra work, we all feel more secure. We are still sailing so fast that it requires a lot of work to steer. But all agree this is the best sailing any of us has ever enjoyed.

Sixth day out

Today is Phil's birthday and secretly we plan a celebration dinner and party. The morning is spent in weather observations, navigation, and ship's chores. While Phil is on watch, the rest of us, in the cabin, wrap little presents and party favors for tonight. Last night we took aboard seven chunky flying fish, which will make a good celebration meal.

Later we inspect all running rigging for chafe, a daily procedure, and find some on the Jeni-Wing sheets at the stern cheek-blocks. We rig stopper lines, port and starboard, to double up on these sheets in case of failure.

In mid-afternoon we make a second radio report to the National Hurricane Center, and obtain a reassuring weather forecast for the next 72 hours. We also confirm the AMVER plot updating, and ask Neil Frank to telephone our families in Miami reporting our situation and progress.

Seventh day out

Last night we passed "alpha" and made the westerly course change. We had another fast sailing night, with winds averaging 25 knots true. Night watches are still three hours each, dogging every day. This morning we are feeling cumulatively tired and decide this will be a day of rest. The 24-hour run to noon Z today was 185.1 miles through the water, averaging 7.7 knots plus 0.5 knot current. On the new course we steer 280°, compared with a previous 230°. Correcting for 15° of westerly magnetic variation in this part of the ocean, our true course is 265°.

After one week at sea we revel in a complete refreshment of bed linen, towels, and napkins and treat ourselves to hot-water showers. Tonight we move the dinner hour ahead one hour, from 1900 to 1800. This gives us a more cheerful dinner time in daylight. Throughout the voyage we eat all meals at particular hours: breakfast at 0800, lunch at 1230 and dinner now at 1800.

The night of the seventh day was uneventful and we continue fast sailing. *Mischief* is the embodiment of tireless motion and power, as she drives and surges on.

Eighth day out

This is Sunday, but all hands work on chores during the day when time permits, crossing things off the chore list as they are accomplished. At day's end we look back and see only half of the chores done—the urgent ones. Every other day I update and post a new "Ship's Chores—Today" list.

Late afternoon we pass the halfway mark. It is hard to believe we have traveled over 1,500 miles. We realize that if we keep this pace we could make a record crossing of 16 days; it is possible, but not really expected. Seas continue quite lumpy and turbulent; the wind holds steady around 20 knots true. For four consecutive days we have averaged nearly 8 knots speed through the water! We marvel at the seakindliness of the boat's design. Time and again a hump of quartering sea rises above the eye level of the helmsman, overtaking the vessel, but she lifts and drives on with no fuss whatever. Roaring seas that break behind come under her. The boat lifts, surges forward, and settles down a little heavily. Never has she pounded into a sea. When I get home I must be sure to tell Rod Stephens and Frank Kinney about *Mischief*'s fantastic speed, and also to tell Wright Britton, designer of the Jeni-Wings, how pleased we are with these sails.

Ninth day out

At 0510, ten minutes after the change of watch, there is a jarring shock throughout the boat. Then comes the call, "All hands on deck!" The off-watch crew rushes out on deck. First Phil, then Gayle, while I struggle doggedly below in blasphemous conflict with a zipper. Meanwhile, to clear the cockpit for action, Gayle spots two empty coffee cups and tosses them below onto my bunk, only to find one half-full of cold coffee. After these initial false starts, we turn to the job at hand.

The foredeck floodlight reveals a wildly flapping set of Jeni-Wings, some of it overboard and the rest burying the deck in a confusion of nylon. The halyard has parted and lies coiled like a snake of wire and rope on deck. Under bare poles we steer downwind, not wanting to start the engine in case any lines are in the water. While Gayle steers, three of us work calmly and cautiously at damage control for over an hour and a half. When finished, the precious Wings are safely in a sailbag lashed in position on deck, the broken halyard coiled, taped, and stowed, and all sheets and lines coiled and secured in place. We put up the staysail and elect to run with this alone, as the wind and seas are increasing. But the motion of the boat is unpleasant and quick, and the boat rolls severely at times.

At breakfast, the main topics of conversation are the causes of the failure, how to avoid repetition, the possibility of damage to the Wings, and the procedure for stopping the now unfurled sails before hoisting them on another halyard. After breakfast we dump the billowing 1,100 square feet of sail on its twisted coil of roller-furling luff wire below into the cabin for inspection. It spreads from the forepeak to the after cabin with great piles at both ends. Careful examination reveals only one place requiring repair, a tear of about two feet in a seam.

This is no time for an amateur stitch; we select a locked herringbone stitch, and Gayle and I, taking turns with the needle and palm, complete the repair in about two hours. By mid-afternoon we are ready to rerig. We are a little hesitant, as the weather is threatening and perhaps the wind is blowing too hard to risk a hoisting foul-up. We decide to postpone the operation.

To balance the boat better, without using the mainsail, we put up the storm trysail and carry it with the staysail. This results in a very uncomfortable night of deep rolling at 6 knots.

Tenth day out

The first thing this morning we put up the Wings, and what a difference! Again the motion of the boat is subdued and rhythmic and she leaps ahead in speed. The past day's run of 108 miles reflects yesterday's slow going; today she will do better. This is a weather-reporting day. Our crew has faithfully recorded the weather despite distractions. But I spend two unproductive and frustrating hours at the radio in an unsuccessful attempt to reach WOM in Miami, and finally give up.

Eleventh day out

A metallic squeak is heard at the stemhead fitting of the Wings. Mac comes forward with some oil and is astounded to find a fresh pile of bronze shavings around the pad eye to which the stainless steel shackle holding the Jeni-Wing furling drum is attached. The pad eye is sheared halfway through and ready to burst open any second!

We quickly furl the Wings and drop the halyard. The next six hours are spent removing the strongly fastened pad eye. After a shipwide search for the spare fails, we "borrow" one from another part of the deck and replace it at the stemhead. We then inspect all sheets and fittings for other chafe and once more get the Wings up and flying.

To keep the foredeck clear of the staysail we have been under power and the boat is rolling heavily. To work and hold on at the same time is a strain. Gayle has steered all day so the three men could accomplish the task as quickly as possible. By late afternoon we are tired but pleased to have the Wings flying again. It is said that in any long passage chafe may be a ship's greatest enemy; we could not contradict this ancient maxim.

To conserve energy after our unscheduled chores, we decide to relax, and for the second day we postpone our scheduled weather report. This is a calculated risk, because if six days elapse after a scheduled reporting day without word from us, AMVER will radio an urgent advisory to all ships to be on the lookout for us.

Twelfth day out

We are rolling off longitude now since our turn at alpha, and today the ship's clocks are set back one hour to ZD +3. We have been trying unsuccessfully to receive United States Observatory time ticks, having sailed out of range of BBC in our westing. Today we finally made contact on the Zenith Transoceanic radio, receiving time from Denver, Colorado. The ship's quartz chronometer is twelve seconds fast, evidently due to human error when the batteries were recently replaced.

We are now in the tropics; winds are balmy, and we shed our clothes even at night. Occasionally we need more ventilation below, so we dig out two of the four ventilators, buried deep in the lazarette, and install them on deck. Air and sea temperatures have both risen to an average of 76° F. Two weeks ago sea temperature was 63°, air 64°.

It is hard to believe we have been under way nearly two weeks, sailing night and day. The time seems much shorter in our comfortable daily routine. This is a weather-reporting day, and in mid-afternoon we make clear radio contact with Miami. We call in our observations and hear that the State Department advises aborting the Grenada landfall because of a serious local disorder. After discussion on the radio, I accept this advice and ask that AMVER be notified of the change in our sailing plan. We will head for Barbados instead of Grenada, altering course in two days for a northwesterly reach. We are now below latitude 12° North and sliding a little more south than I would like in order to carry the Jeni-Wings full. I think we are also making some leeway. Grenada lies 12° North, Barbados about 13° North. The distance to Barbados from here is about 850 miles; at 175 miles per day we might expect arrival in five days.

We take the Wings down for chafe inspection, happily finding none. Since one halyard parted, we have been

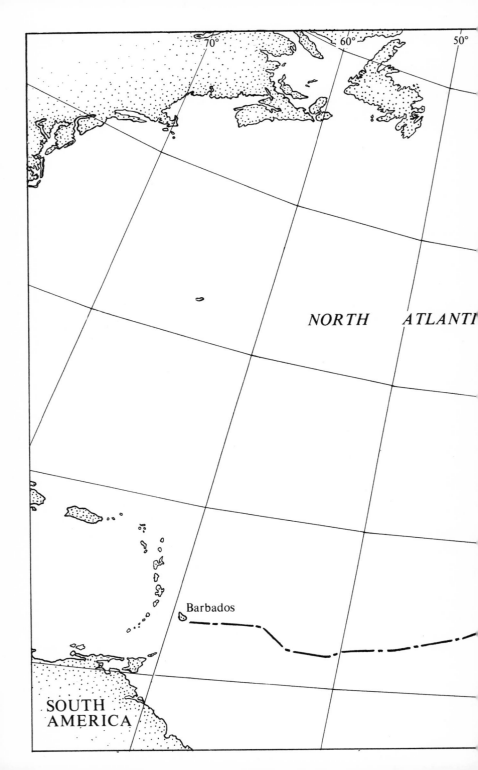

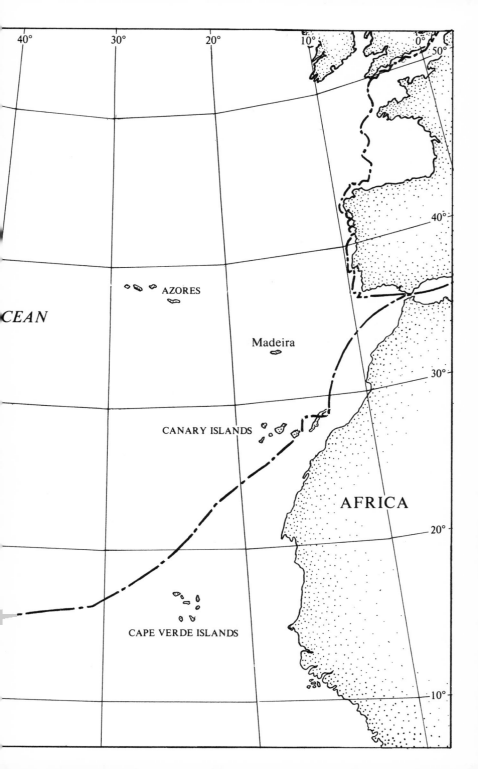

greasing the first five feet of the plow-steel #2 halyard as a precaution against chafe at the masthead sheave.

An afternoon running fix again puts us south and east of our DR position. We are disappointed not to find ourselves as far along or as far north as we thought. We guess that ocean currents are not giving us the expected 0.5-knot westerly drift. (We learned on arrival that other yachts experienced the same phenomenon.)

Mischief keeps sailing, sailing, lurching, gently rolling, driving, surging, settling in a great frothy bed, then repeating the cycle.

Fourteenth and fifteenth days out

The last two daily runs are among our best; we sail 173 miles through the water our fifteenth day, an average of 7.2 knots. That evening we take a round of stars. Gayle tape records the entire procedure, which proves very interesting in replay. We obtain a good three-star fix, plot it, and decide that tomorrow we will change course to accomplish the necessary northing for Barbados. It is too bad that this hike will spoil our near-record crossing for a boat our size by adding more than a day to the passage time.

Sixteenth day out

This morning we change sails and course as planned. Weather is favorable. The new course of 330° is approximately northwest true. Speed is around 7 knots or better with reefed main, staysail, and mizzen. *Mischief* is a bit active but steers well. Today we set the ship's clock back another hour, the fourth time en route. We are now in time zone +4, the same as Miami EDT and Barbados local time.

With the radio direction finder I try to reach a land radio beacon without success. We are puzzled by the fact that we have run out our distance from Gran Canaria and still appear to be 300 miles southeast of Barbados. Last night the ship's electronic Harrier Log turned 10,000 sea miles since *Mischief*'s commissioning, July, 1972.

Small things can cause big troubles, or irritations, as is well known. This afternoon we lost one of the small shackles halfway up the luff of the mainsail, causing a high-frequency flutter and drumming against the metal mast. I climb the ladder with a replacement shackle but simply cannot put it in place with one hand. We take the big sail down for this small repair. While it is down we decide to use the storm trysail for the night, instead of the main, as the wind is dropping and the main boom may slat badly in light air. In this undercanvassed rig we have a slow, unpleasant night of rolling and bucking. Frequently seas slam onto *Mischief*'s side and douse the cockpit or an open hatch or port.

Seventeenth day out

We are doggedly northing and now have covered about 120 miles by DR. The going is uncomfortable, and we can hardly wait to get the Wings flying again. To have a little "money in the bank" when we turn and run for Barbados, we should reach into 13° 30' North. A morning sun sight position advanced to a noon meridian passage line confirms our DR position a bit north of the thirteenth parallel. By 1300 hours the Wings are flying again and we are off on our final course, headed for the barn! The ship becomes quiet and stable, the water gurgles by as speed increases to 7 knots in a light breeze. We head for South Point, Barbados, approximately 240 miles distant. Our ETA is midnight tomorrow. This raises the question of whether to enter at night or stand off for daylight. Our Carlisle Bay destination is open and uncomplicated, so we will enter in whatever light there is and anchor in front of the Barbados Yacht Club.

The 24-hour run to noon Z today reflects poor time made last night under the shortened rig and lumpy seas, only 124 miles through the water for an average of 5.1

211

knots. That our ETA is the night of the eighteenth day gives us a glow of pride in a fast passage. The average for boats of the 40′ to 45′ size is apparently 21 days. An unofficial record is 16 days, made a few years ago by a 42-footer. We are passing a quiet day, sometimes with light wind. By sundown our DR position is 200 miles east of Barbados.

Eighteenth day out

Soon after dawn there is a short tropical rainfall, the first rain encountered on the voyage. It makes us feel that we are getting close to land. We see land birds flying east this morning, another sign that land is near. Land birds feeding at sea fly upwind in the morning, returning downwind in the evening.

The latest day's run through the water is 135 miles, an average of 5.6 knots. This is not bad, but nothing like the fast days earlier in the voyage. After several attempts during the last 24 hours, I finally pick up the Seawell Aero Beacon on Barbados, finding it on the starboard bow as indeed it should be. It is a beautiful day; we are sailing comfortably, but not especially fast. The ETA is advanced to mid-morning tomorrow.

The weather team has taken a final round of weather observations for transmission tomorrow. It is hard to believe we are so close to our destination after such a long voyage. It seems that this sailing could go on forever, so far as our physical condition and the still-eager vessel are concerned. Food and water are the only limiting factors, and we have almost enough of these remaining aboard to make another trip across the ocean.

The awareness that land is not far away brings with it a number of thoughts: anticipation of the landfall and things to do ashore, assuredly, but also a reluctance to end the voyage. Then there is the navigational hazard of closing with the land. Land is a boat's enemy; in fact, the most dangerous part of the trip lies ahead. The night-watch is doubled, and the whole ship is alert.

Nineteenth day out

Landfall is slow to develop. Since 0100 last night each of us has expected to see the island on the western horizon, particularly as there are two seacoast lights having 30-mile visibility. Now in daylight we calculate that Barbados' highest elevation of 1,100 feet should be visible from 40 miles away. Our DR is run out and we should be in sight of land. In this tense moment I find comfort in a guidebook's comment. It refers to the flat terrain of Barbados and the difficulty local sailors have in sighting it, quoting a West Indian schooner captain returning from Grenada: "Barbados done sunk! We was whar she is an' she ain't der no mo'!"

Then at 1023, standing on the bridge deck with glasses, I make out the gray outline of heights of land on the starboard bow through the haze that has been obscuring our view. Phil at the helm confirms this. Here is our landfall, after 3,176 miles of open ocean!

We give South Point a two-mile berth to clear offshore reefs safely. I reach the Miami Hurricane Center on the radio to transmit our weather observations while still at sea. They congratulate us on successful completion of the voyage and upon the high quality of our weather observation reports. It pleases us to be asked to make future reports at sea at our discretion (and their expense).

At 1405 we furl the powerful Jeni-Wings, and with staysail, mizzen, and motor we alter course to round into Carlisle Bay. At 1615 the hook is down.

A 40' customs launch comes bumping alongside, and formalities are quickly and politely completed. We swim in the crystal clear tropical water and enjoy our first real happy hour in 19 days.

Then we row ashore in the rubber dinghy for the

traditional "Captain's dinner." It is now twilight, and we discover there is no place to land the dinghy except through the surf. With howls of laughter we manage this and soak our clean shore clothes in the process. Such is our first touch of land.

The voyage is over so suddenly. One moment we are secure in a familiar daily routine. Suddenly everything is changed, changed to an environment of unaccustomed sights, sounds, smells, and movement. We miss the motion of the boat, the wind in our faces, the fresh smells and exhilaration of the open sea.

Of course we are proud that we have successfully completed such a fine voyage, and are thankful for a safe trip, good weather, fast, glorious sailing, and our good health. Indeed, we are grateful for the whole experience.

This transatlantic voyage has been an experience of a lifetime for each of us. Although no doubt we will repeat it on other seas in the future, nothing could equal the thrill, the satisfaction, and the adventure of our first major ocean crossing in our own remarkable vessel.